T0258232

THE DIALOGUES

Gnoondiwinan

Also by Armand Garnet Ruffo

Poetry and Prose
At Geronimo's Grave
Grey Owl: The Mystery of Archie Belaney
Norval Morrisseau: Man Changing into Thunderbird
Opening in the Sky
The Thunderbird Poems
Treaty #

Film
Jiigishkaand – the Door, short, writer-director
On the Day the World Begins Again, short, writer
A Windigo Tale, feature, writer-director

Anthologies
(Ad)Dressing Our Words: Aboriginal Perspectives on Aboriginal Literatures,
    editor
An Anthology of Canadian Native Literature in English, co-editor
An Anthology of Indigenous Literature in Canada, co-editor
An Introduction to Indigenous Literary Criticism in Canada, co-editor

THE DIALOGUES

Gnoondiwinan

THE SONG OF FRANCIS PEGAHMAGABOW
Gaa-bi-bdikwewdang – Francis Pegahmagabow n'gamwin

ARMAND GARNET RUFFO

Nishnaabemwin translations by Brian D. McInnes
Gaa-aan'kanootmaaged Waabishki-makwa

WOLSAK
& WYNN

© Armand Garnet Ruffo, 2024

Sounding Thunder © Armand Garnet Ruffo, 2018
Nishnaabemwin translation of *Sounding Thunder* © Dr. Brian McInnes, 2024

No part of this publication may be reproduced, stored in a retrieval system or transmitted, in any form or by any means, without the prior written consent of the publisher or a license from the Canadian Copyright Licensing Agency (Access Copyright). For an Access Copyright license, visit www.accesscopyright.ca or call toll free to 1-800-893-5777.

Published by Wolsak and Wynn Publishers
280 James Street North
Hamilton, ON L8R2L3
www.wolsakandwynn.ca

Editor: Noelle Allen | Copy editor: Peter Midgley
Cover and interior design: Jennifer Rawlinson
Cover image: *German Barrage Fire at Night (Ypres)* by Colonel George G. Nasmith
Author photograph: Dai Evans
Typeset in Vendetta, Minion and Calibri
Printed by Rapido Books, Montreal, Canada

10 9 8 7 6 5 4 3 2 1

The publisher gratefully acknowledges the support of the Canada Council for the Arts and the Ontario Arts Council. We also acknowledge the financial support of the Government of Canada through the Canada Book Fund and the Government of Ontario through the Ontario Book Publishing Tax Credit and Ontario Creates.

Library and Archives Canada Cataloguing in Publication

Title: The dialogues : the song of Francis Pegahmagabow / Armand Garnet Ruffo ; Nishnaabemwin translations by Brian D. McInnes = Gnoondiwinan : gaa-bi-bdikwewdang -- Francis Pegahmagabow n'gamwin / Armand Garnet Ruffo ; Gaa-aan'kanootmaaged Waabishki-makwa.
Other titles: Gnoondiwinan : gaa-bi-bdikwewdang -- Francis Pegahmagabow n'gamwin
Names: Ruffo, Armand Garnet, author. | McInnes, Brian D., translator. | Container of (work): Ruffo, Armand Garnet. Sounding thunder. | Container of (expression): Ruffo, Armand Garnet. Sounding thunder. Ojibwa.
Description: Includes the play Sounding Thunder, in English and in Nishnaabemwin translation. | Includes some text in Nishnaabemwin.
Identifiers: Canadiana 20240326172 | ISBN 9781989496916 (softcover)
Subjects: LCSH: Pegahmagabow, Francis, 1891-1952—Poetry. | LCGFT: Poetry.
Classification: LCC PS8585.U514 D53 2024 | DDC C811/.54—dc23

For the Indigenous veterans
and all those thrown into war

CONTENTS / GAA-DGOBII'GA ADEGIN

The War That Will End War

– H.G. Wells, 1914

FAITH ACT
DEBWEWENDMING EN'KAMGAK

SCENE ONE: SETTING THE STAGE – HEREIN THE NARRATOR MAKES HIS APPEARANCE AND IN A STEADY VOICE INTRODUCES FRANCIS PEGAHMAGABOW

PICTURE HIM – male / twenty-five / Anishnaabe-Ojibwe
compact / sturdy / brave / self-reliant / defiant

He steps out of the shadows
and stands quietly
in a distant corner of the trench
In his left hand he holds a pinch of tobacco
that he raises up
to beseech Gitchi-Manido
the Great Mystery

He prays aloud so that the Creator
might hear him
and take pity on him and the company

He begins by honouring the four directions +

*Francis Pegahmagabow wearing service
medals and a Treaty Medal.*

TOGETHER WE FILL THE SPACES BETWEEN

Example One

Short note on pronunciation.
Unless you know something about Anishnaabemowin
you are probably wondering how to pronounce the words.
Sound it out.
Let the vowels roll off your tongue:
Peg-ah-ma-ga-bow.

(Does that help?)

Example Two

20 July 2018. Picture a group of artists sitting around portable banquet
tables at the Wasauksing community centre for a feast to welcome us.
This is our first major production, and we are nervous. We are here
in Francis Pegahmagabow's home community on Parry Island,
the second largest island in the Georgian Bay archipelago.
Family members, along with Chief Wally Tabobondung and
the council, are here to bear witness. Tim Corlis, the composer,
will later tell me that those of us who were part of the creative process
understood that everything was riding on this premiere.
We had written the work for two audiences, Indigenous and settler,
and we understood that the reception here from Francis's descendants
and their community would be a defining moment for it.
If they had any serious issues with what we had done,
Sounding Thunder: The Song of Francis Pegahmagabow
would come crashing down
like one of the huge bronze cymbals in the production.

3

We begin with belief.

A FEW WORDS ABOUT THE WESTERN FRONT IN THE SPRING OF 1915 TO ADD TO THE VOLUMES ALREADY IN PRINT (OR IS THAT THE PEN OF THE NARRATOR'S NARRATOR YOU HEAR SCRATCHING IN FUTILITY?)

A trench of mud and blood and piss and shit. Dawn unlike any you have ever witnessed. The scene is one of desolation. Everything as far as the eye can see, ruin. Trees blasted into mere skeletons of their former green selves, homes a pile of rubble, your comrades like the blasted trees, mere ghosts of their former lives.

The sky eternally grey.

The sounds you hear are hoarse whispers, coughing, hacking, muttering, constant moaning, the glass-eyed wounded, their limbs torn off, the half bodies, the shell-shocked, the insane, whimpering to themselves to everyone and anyone. In the distance rumbling of the big guns. Constant. Pitiless. Relentless artillery . . . fire . . . fire . . . fire.

A flare arcs across the grey sky, illuminating it for a few seconds.

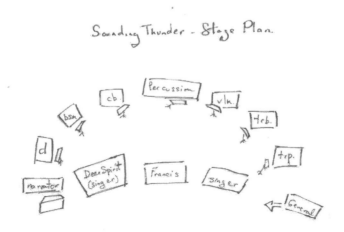

Waabanokwe, Waabanong genawendang.

Zhaawanogiizhig, Zhaawanong genawendang

Nenabozh, Ebangishimog genawendang

Giiwedin, Giiwedinong genawendang.

keeper
Wabenokkwe, ~~master~~ of the east.

keeper
Shauwanigizik, ~~ruler~~ of the south.

keeper
Nanabush, ~~guardian~~ of the west.

keeper
Giyuedin, ~~spirit~~ of the north.

Translations can never be exact. In her novel *Fugitive Pieces*, a book mired in war, Anne Michaels writes that reading a poem in translation is like kissing a woman through a veil. You never quite get it. She refers to the difficulty of translating Greek poetry. What about Anishnaabemowin? Linguists consider it one of the most complex languages on the planet. Six thousand verb forms. A reflection of a peoples' reality.

SCENE TWO: CALL TO ACTION – HEREIN FRANCIS PEGAHMAGABOW IS SINGLED OUT AND ORDERED TO PERFORM A MIRACLE

The war has been raging
on the Western Front.
for less than a year.

And thanks to new technology,
machine guns, tanks, airplanes,
long-range artillery,
tens of thousands of soldiers
have already died in the slaughter.

Millions more will follow.
Any thought of a quick end
is mired in mud and blood.
To break the stalemate
the enemy turns to a new killing tool: chlorine gas.
And the Canadians are without masks.

According to official records of the department [of Indian Affairs] more than four thousand Indians enlisted for active service with the Canadian Expeditionary forces. It must be remembered, moreover, that there were undoubtedly cases of Indian enlistment which were not reported.

— D.C. Scott, Deputy Superintendent General
of the Department of Indian Affairs,
"The Canadian Indians and the Great World War," 1919

A STIFF UPPER LIP IS REQUIRED TO CARRY ON

WWI becomes the first industrialized war.

Up to this point the world has never experienced
anything like it. Until then soldiers ride horses.
Parade them. March in formation. Horse nations
spring up on the great plains and become synonymous
with the Comanche, Kiowa, Apache, Blackfoot, Cree,
who become renowned for their horsemanship.
Warriors track on horses. Attack on horses. Live on horses.

In this future nightmare soldiers find themselves
riding and marching into a spray of .30 calibre
machine gun bullets that tear them to pieces in seconds.
Airplanes raze the ground. Aerial bombing.[1]
Tanks and artillery the likes of never seen before.
As for horses, they become relegated to transport and
lie dead in the fields. Eyes blank. Flies buzzing overhead.

1 "During World War I, aircraft were first used for surveillance purposes, but by 1915 they were increasingly used in offensive operations." *Encyclopedia Britannica*, s.v. "strategic bombing," accessed May 7, 2024, www.britannica.com/topic/strategic -bombing. A Good God Note: Despite international humanitarian law, it has since become standard practice to aerial bomb civilians and civilian infrastructure, such as hospitals and schools, as witnessed in the dark soul of every subsequent war.

9

The first attack creates havoc.
General Edwin Alderson is desperate

He approaches Francis Pegahmagabow
who is crouched at the edge of the trench
oiling the breech mechanism of his Ross rifle.

The men have been talking about you, ~~he barks~~.

Francis jumps to attention. Yes, Sir.

He stares straight ahead
into the horde of men and horses
moving weapons and supplies.

Is it true you can change the wind's direction?

The general asks this in a lower register
so that others will not overhear
his strange question. He is concerned
how this may appear.

For a moment Francis does not know how to respond.
It occurs to him that the men must have seen him
praying.

I can try, he says, looking the general in the face.

Alright do it, Alderson commands.

The general turns on his heels and leaves
as quickly as he arrived.

DIMENSIONAL INTERLUDE

Another Faded Historical – Take Your Pick – Personal Account

by 1915 the damn war is not going as planned
Lieutenant-General E.A.H. Alderson
– in fact it's a mess
a battle-hardened British general
loyal to a fault
assumes command
a bite as big as his bark
of the 1st Canadian Division when it
is getting hot under the collar
arrives in England in October 1914 he takes them to France
see him stare grimly into the camera, daring you
in 1915 and commands the brutal, confused fighting
to see him, I mean *really* see him
at the Second Battle of Ypres, outgunned,
he appears like a man in trouble
outnumbered and facing the first lethal chlorine gas attacks
or a troubled man – slice it as you will
in the history of warfare, the division defends the Ypres Salient
he is a man who lets you see
the cost 6,000 killed, wounded and missing.
only what he wants
Alderson is later removed from of the Canadian Corps
you to see
after the disastrous Battle of St. Eloi, another
not what
1,400 young dead and dying
you see

Change the wind?

The general wonders

if what he asks

so curious and strange

is not indeed a sin.

A LAPSE OF WEIGHT AND MEASURE

The anthropologist exhumes the bones of origin
and licks her lips in a question.
I don't believe it, she says. It's all too musty.

Then there is the astrophysicist who cuts a fine figure
looking through absence a billion galaxies away
all the earnestness of computational analysis.

Meanwhile in a white room you see only on a screen
the medical researcher straps down his struggling specimen
and moves to the extremities of feeling.

Cut to the arborist pruning the day
where the weeping willow weeps blood and milk in a language
she tries to decode.

As for us, our options are laid out on a table
centred somewhere between death and acceptance
– or fear and our latest purchase.

Isn't it incomprehensible, all those things
that make comprehension melt
like Dalí's clocks?

Without inhaling the tobacco
Francis makes his offering
and asks the wind guardians
to overtake the gas.

Spiritual order provides guidance
he puts tobacco down
on the earth
to give prayers
of humility and rebirth.

Just before sunrise the wind changes
from east to west,
and the Germans suffer
just as much as the Allies do.

Like the Geté nishnaabeg,
the Indians of old,
Francis's offering is accepted
and heard by the spirit world.

Chi-Miigwech Gitchi Manido.

Translation. Geté = Old, ancient, former . . . ancient Indians.

— Bishop Frederic Baraga, *A Dictionary of the Otchipwe Language,* 1853

(Problem. No reference to ancient knowledge in the translation.)

HOW TO INTERPRET AN INTERPRETATION

Kissed by a (Christian) Translation

Manito, spirit, ghost
Mino-manito, the good spirit [notice, not God]
Matchi-manito, the evil spirit, the devil [notice, Devil]
Manitowiwin, quality or character of spirit [either-or]

— Bishop Frederic Baraga, *A Dictionary of the Otchipwe Language,* 1853

SCENE THREE: BACKGROUND – HEREIN THE REEL ROLLS BACKWARDS – BIRTH AND DEATH IF ANYTHING ARE DRAMATIC

Born in 1889, Francis Pegahmagabow
    an Ojibwe boy, is now age two
and like any other boy
    unaware of what
he will go on to do,
    but dark clouds appear
on his horizon, upheaval
    the height of mountainous waves,
grave enough to change
    the course of a child's life:
his father dies,
    his mother gravely ill,
an adopted grandfather raises the boy,
    teaches him ceremony,
custom and tradition.

Shaped by glory days of old
    quest and vision
the sickly child takes it upon himself
    to entreat the help
of the Sun Manido.
    He rises at dawn
and runs from village
    to shoreline, training
to be warrior strong.

There is the dream always the same dream

of a life tested

a life lived

inaadiziwin

fully

THE NARRATOR'S NARRATOR CLEARS HIS THROAT

Where all creation (we) rests on the back of the strongest (you)
and depends on the grasp of the weakest (they),
and all is related.

What does this mean exactly
and more importantly
what does it mean to (us?) Try.

Questions abound
in breath and thought,
afflict him
like a cold winter night
when the fire is low

And so he asks,
what does it mean
to be a good man
a brave man
a kind and honourable man?
Who will help
save his people
lest they perish
blown to the four directions?

His beliefs a way of the past
his language gone
deeper than the realm
of Nzaagimaa,
chief of the water serpents

vanished with the generations.

REMEMBER YOU ARE HEARING MUSIC

Instrumentation

Bb Clarinet (doubles on A)

Bassoon

Bb Trumpet (doubles on piccolo trumpet D or Bb)

Trombone

Violin

Contrabass

Percussion:
D Handpan, Vibes, Suspended Cymbals (medium & large), Bass Drum,
Floor Tom, Side Drum, Snare Drum,
Mark Tree, Woodblock

A SHORT INTERLUDE #1

Two Indians go into a bar. Have you heard it?

One of them has just enfranchised to get a job
with the Department of Lands and Forests.
Cheers, he says to his buddy
clanking his glass.
Today I am no longer an Indian.

True story.

A Victorian world, Canada.
Indians can't work. Indians can't vote.
Unless they enfranchise and lose their treaty rights,
pretend not to be Indian.
Until 1960 when Prime Minister
Dief-the-Chief
dons a headdress.
Swear that's what they used to call him.

True story.

The boy now a young man

sees that he must challenge

and do battle where battle is due.

Strength and deed becoming one

he becomes the voice of

SOUNDING THUNDER

A SHORT SWEET NOTE ON COLLABORATION

Tim and I worked seamlessly together, telephoning and emailing
each other constantly. He would send me a piece of music, and
I would work on the libretto.
I had already done the research and had the storyline in mind,
and so it became a question of feeling it in my body
and getting the words to fit the music,
much like a jigsaw puzzle I suppose. The most important thing
I learned is that a libretto has to give the music
enough room to soar.

SCENE FOUR: A SPIRITUAL ENCOUNTER – HEREIN FRANCIS HAS AN UNEXPECTED ENCOUNTER WITH HIS DEER SPIRIT

FRANCIS
In my dream
I see a beautiful deer,
head raised,
nose up, ears twitching.
I approach from downwind,
but it turns to me,
and I realize
this is meant to be.
It is a spirit,
a Manido –
in the body of a deer.

I know who you are.

DEER SPIRIT
And so you do. I am your relative.

FRANCIS
Pegahmagabow, Caribou clan.

DEER SPIRIT
Gentle and swift,
and yet strong
and made to defend,
these qualities
in the body of a man.
Know that you have kin,
human
and other-than-human,
to help you on your life path
do it now,
be done with the task.

Francis Aims His Rifle. He Cannot Bring Himself to Shoot.

ROOTS OF A NAME

Pegahmagabow ← Begamigaabaw → (translation) Standing Storm

- - - - - - - - - - - - - You know what this means if you have been paying attention.

WHY THE DEER SPIRIT

What became clear to me as my roots grew and
I came into consciousness upon thinking and listening
to elders and artists and thinkers over the years
was that the newcomers to Turtle Island encountered
a belief system so far outside of Western philosophical tradition
that it was unrecognizable to them. In their ignorance
they quickly dismissed it as primitive and without purpose
or worth, and in doing so they dismissed an ancient body
of knowledge about the natural world that Indigenous people
worldwide have drawn upon to find connection to all
living things – a fundamental ethos defining our space
and place in the world.
We are currently living or better to say non-living
with the consequences of this rejection.

FRANCIS   I need to bring home food.
               I know what it is like
               to nearly starve.

DEER SPIRIT   I am Ogimâ
               spirit chief of the deer
               I give myself to you in this way.

               Do what you must do.

Francis Struggles to Press the Trigger. He Finally Does It.

A PERSONAL NOTE

When I was a boy complaining about the food
at the dinner table, stew again, my mother told me
that after her grandfather died
she and her grandmother lived on rabbits.

I knew rabbits, I snared them.
I listened to their squeaky little voices
as I wrung their necks.
After that I ate whatever was on my plate.

A NOTE ON ETYMOLOGY

Ogimâ. Chief, chieftain, superior agent, officer.
(Meaning power, leadership.)

– Bishop Frederic Baraga, *A Dictionary of the Otchipwe Language*, 1853

[ADDENDUM
An old word little used today.]

Travelling home
        with enough meat
to feed hungry bellies
        the snow path breaks loose
and Francis loses his stride
        tumbles down
onto a frozen lake
        where he lies.
A mighty crack issues
        and down he goes
through the ice
        and into the frigid
water.

A WORD FROM OUR NARRATOR'S NARRATOR WHO SEES ALL AND YET KEEPS TRIPPING UP ON PHYSICAL MATTER SLIPPERY AS A RUG FULL OF HOLES

We can say Francis's story
hinges on the spiritual.
(War can mark a life and still be incidental.)
It is difficult to mention Spirit these days
unless you are talking to the old or young,
greed and excess the life-
style for the middle middling.

Example Three

Last year a couple bought the empty lot next door to
my writing shed near Haliburton and cut down basically every tree,
including a sweet stand of maple – leaving only
the few required by law – and built a 3,500 sq. (estimating) ft.
glass mansion with a gravelled parking lot
the size of an airfield. This year flipped,
asking price $1,349,000.00 (not estimating).

Spirituality today is synonymous
with organized religion
in turn associated with atrocity
global imperialism on a large scale
holocaust after holocaust
scandal after scandal
at the local level
then there's the religious far right
conjuring images of politicians
and religious leaders
wrapped in intolerance, bigotry,
self-serving nihilism
behind gated and gilded walls

I know what you're thinking, too on the nose. But, hey,
I stayed up half the night listening to their humongous
jet-taking-off air conditioner.

There's a war out there.

DEER SPIRIT   Though you believe your death is near
               and sing a brave song
               to allay your fear
               it is not ours to predict
               when our time has come.

               I, guardian Manido
               benevolent spirit
               bid you to move back
               into the light of the sun.
               With a wave a turtle shall rise
               as though carrying the world.

               Your feet now planted
               firmly on its back,
               with a shake of his shell
               he throws you up and out
               as light as a snowflake
               falling about the shore.

FRANCIS   I awake in the snow,
                                    dazed
               and I brush myself off.
               I think my feet must have landed
                                              on rock
               and I leapt
               with all my caribou strength.

In the Indigenous worldview, all Creation is sacred and
spirituality alive. As one Elder described it, once a person
set foot outside his lodge, the entire world is his church.
Land is a living entity that must be treated with respect.
Spirituality is to be practiced daily rather than merely written
about or practiced in a rigid institutional setting. Underlying all
Aboriginal beliefs is a view of a world gifted by Manitow.
Our purpose on earth is to develop an understanding
of how to live in harmony
with all of Creation.

— Blair Stonechild, *The Knowledge Seeker*, 2016

Example Four

A few years ago I went to an exhibition at the Ontario Art Gallery
titled *Anthropocene*. It consisted of photographs by Edward Burtynsky,
including large murals augmented by film extensions by Jennifer Baichwal
and Nicholas de Pencier. A description of the exhibit told us the artists
travelled to countries on every continent, save Antarctica, documenting
irreversible marks of human activity. Informed by scientific research,
powered by aesthetic vision and inspired by a desire to bear **witness**,
the images revealed the scale and gravity of our impact on the planet.

It was nicely explained but the reality of seeing the artists' vision
was a different matter. There was a fundamental contradiction
that the viewer could **not escape**. You felt it at the very core of
your being. It held you in its seductive gaze. The aesthetics of
the images were magnificent: colour, tone, contrast, detail,
but this impeccable beauty could only last for a moment
because the viewer was witnessing the destruction humankind
has wreaked on the earth. Neither Dante's *Inferno* nor
Bruegel's *Death* had anything on these horrific scenes of **war**
against the very planet that **sustains** us.

What have we done? That was the cry I saw on everyone's face
as they too turned away, unable to hold their gaze,
our **fear** and **helplessness** palpable.

Francis Is Back in His Village Home.

FRANCIS   When they press me
about spiritual matters
I shrug as though in half belief,
I don't argue or fight.

I seek balance
in a world both ancient
and modern.
I press for support
to go to school
and learn to play the cornet
in a local brass band.

I'm twenty-one years old and free
living in a new century,
and I sign on as a seaman
to travel the Great Lakes.

Francis Pegahmagabow on Parry Island.

Turn of the twentieth century. Francis is a modern man
living in two worlds. Think for a minute what is going on
in early twentieth-century modernism. The first mapping of the gene,
the chromosome, Einstein's Theory of General Relativity,
Picasso's Blue Period (dulled to *Guernica*'s monochromatic vision
of war), Kandinsky's *Blue Rider* movement, Jelly Roll Morton's
"Jelly Roll Blues," Armstrong picking the horn and turning it
into Fitzgerald's Jazz Age,
Josephine tearing up the dance floor.
It's all happening.

(Meanwhile in the capital of Canada, a small provincial town,
D.C. Scott, an equally small man with big literary aspirations,
makes residential school for Indians mandatory.
The government department controls their every move
enforces a policy of pass laws. The language. The pipe.
The drum. The Sweat Lodge. All banned. In their place: Poverty.
Prison. Addiction. Joblessness. Homelessness
Discrimination. Segregation. Assimilation.
As for Francis, he does his best to sidestep it -------------------- All
it's happening.)

SCENE FIVE: POWER – HEREIN WE SEE FRANCIS'S MODERN LIFE SHAKEN AS HE DRAWS ON HIS TRADITIONS FOR UNDERSTANDING

Francis Waves a Greeting and Approaches a Family of Ojibwe.

That summer they dock near Thunder Bay,
and he joins a band of Ojibwe
picking blueberries by the shore.
He tells them his clan,
and they are the same,
and they welcome him,
share food and tell stories.
It is only when the Thunderbirds roar
that they say goodbye
and go their way,
but not before
an old Medicine Man among them
speaks.

TO NOT KNOW IS EXTREMELY DIFFICULT TO COMPREHEND WHEN YOU HAVE BEEN TRAINED TO KNOW EVERYTHING

In school at the back of the class staring out the window I learned
early that Indians were looked on as inferior, primitive, ignorant,
a burden, an impediment to the settler's concept of civilization.

For the longest time we just kept our heads down or dropped out.
But now the planet has turned her broken heart to us.

FOR THE LAST FEW HUNDRED COLOSSAL NORTH ATLANTIC RIGHT WHALES

What will we say about you when you are gone
will we say that in your dominion you were royalty,
majestic in your element, elemental in your nature
will we shroud your passing in requiem and sing
that you were the one who would rise like an aqueous
star, explode, and then instantly plunge fathoms
below where stillness bubbled creation, will we write
that you were the stuff of story by an ambitious author
who dreamed you in black ink, pitting you against
the darkest shadow of humanity, will we lament
that you were such a godly sight to behold,
riding light as a tall ship rides a wave, though
with far more grace and ease for you were both light
and wave, will we say in our unending shame
in the end you became but an object, a cartoon absence
spouting water up to balloon clouds forever and never
to be witnessed again (?) Will we?

SHAMAN   Listen to the sounds above.
             In one year's time such thundering you will hear
             and in grave danger you shall be,
             but do not fear for I have something for you.
             This medicine has come down from generations past
             and holds the power
             to protect you
             when you think all is lost.

FRANCIS   Chi-Miigwetch, thank you
             so much for your gift.
             I am honoured
             and will wear it
             wherever I go.

Francis Touches the Medicine Pouch Around His Neck.

AN INTERLUDE TO DISCUSS FRANCIS'S ENCOUNTER

Traditional spiritualism among Anishnaabek is both simple and complex. There is no Church, no priest or minister, but there is a lodge, there are knowledge keepers or spiritual leaders and there is a systematic organization of belief. It is not random or haphazard. One enters the lodge in a specific direction, just as one exits it.

It is orderly in the way it follows the natural elements, the cardinal directions, the sun rising, the sun setting, the natural life forces that sustain us like fire and water. One can say it honours the life that gives us life through ritual and ceremony and holding it all together is a pantheon of spiritual forces representing human behaviour and the natural world, all in a sacred relationship and with layer upon layer of story teachings.

By the turn of the nineteenth century traditional ceremonies on reserves like Wasauksing were banned and in southern communities especially kept under the watchful eye of the Indian Agent and the police. Furthermore, the missionaries were among the very first to arrive on reserves, making Christianity a prominent presence and political force, the various denominations vying with each other to claim souls.

When Francis meets the Shaman in remote northern Ontario free from the watchful eye of authority, his modern Christian-influenced self would likely have been surprised but Francis, unlike many, did not attend a residential school and was raised with the old stories and taught to speak Anishnaabemowin. Accordingly, he understands innately the spiritual power, the Manidoowiwin, in the encounter.

That he shared the same clan (Caribou) as the Shaman (whose name is unrecorded) gives him further connection and, in a sense, it opens a door for him that he chooses to walk through – nothing in relation to Anishinaabek spiritually is forced – and it affects him profoundly. To his dying day Francis believed his encounter with the Shaman he met in Rossport saved his life, and the experience remained with him. He took it to heart.

It makes no difference what men think of war, said the judge. . . .
War was always here. Before man was, war waited for him.
The ultimate trade awaiting its ultimate practitioner.

– Cormac McCarthy, *Blood Meridian*, 1985

WAR ACT
GCHI-MIIGAADWIN EN'KAMGAK

SCENE ONE: ENLISTING – HEREIN FRANCIS RATIONALIZES WHY HE AND SO MANY OTHER ANISHNAABEK FEEL COMPELLED TO ENLIST

Francis Stands in Front of a Recruiting Officer.

>   Then he's back on his island home
>   in time to witness
>   the beginning
>   of the darkest unknown,
>   the greatest crime:
>   when reason is abandoned
>   to mankind's folly,
>   and the great circle of life
>   reflecting the promise of youth
>   is shattered.
>   August 1914. Great Britain
>   and Germany are at war,
>   and within days Francis
>   and thousands
>   of other young men
>   enlist.

OFFICER   Let me get this straight,
you insist on fighting a war that's not yours?

>   The officer looks him over
>   begrudgingly
>   and would rather
>   send the Indian on his way.
>   But all the same
>   Francis digs his heels in
>   and explains
>   why he and so many of his people,
>   feel compelled
>   to do their part.

In 1812 a war party from the [Nipigon] reserve paddled the entire
length of Lake Superior and proceeded to Queenston Heights,
where it joined the forces of General Brock.

– D.C. Scott, Deputy Superintendent General
of the Department of Indian Affairs,
"The Canadian Indians and the Great World War," 1919

HIDDEN HISTORY, 1812

– in the beat of the drum in the roll of the lake – paddle
– when singing is the sound and the sound is the song – paddle
– of the water off the water of the wave off the wave – paddle
– when the rhythm is the rhythm of the dip and the pull – paddle
– of the wind and the sun of the rain and the cloud – paddle
– in the arm in the muscle in the shoulder in the breath – paddle
– in the power in the spirit in the knife in the bow – paddle
– in the being and the knowing in the living and the dead – paddle
– for our land for our home for our family for our nation – paddle
– in our truth and our courage in our duty in our honour – paddle
– paddle . . . . paddle . . . . paddle
to war
we

FRANCIS   It's my duty to serve king and country
           for there can be no denying the treaties
           my people made
           with Britain
           shall stand
           the test of time,
           now and forever,
           allies, nation to nation.

                   A history that has gone unaware
                   creates a pensive silence
                   between the two men
                   harkens back to distant times
                   other wars
                   and other enemies on native land
                   when Indian allies
                   swept down on rivers
                   and changed the tide
                   the making of borders
                   the creation of a country.

A SHORT HISTORY OF WAR

Maybe begin with the Romans who turned killing
into a tactical art. Eight centuries before Christ
six centuries after, and they were still at it.
Or maybe start earlier with the Peloponnesian War.
Athens and Sparta a stone's throw apart and
their hands around each other's throat
to be top dog in the playground. Poor Athens.
Poor Sparta. Nobody wins forever. Then
there's that colossal statue of Genghis Khan
perched on horseback, marching across
the Mongolian plain. Legend has it
he personally murdered millions, his army beheading
a whole city at one sitting. Always somebody clubbing
somebody. Brings me to the first big scene
in Kubrick's *2001: A Space Odyssey*,
an ape takes his first swing with a jawbone
– and there we have it
our own voracious perpetual-motion machine
the mechanism of death and suffering.
No stopping it.

A SNIPER KILLS OR GETS KILLED

We have been in the trenches. I just got initiated
by German bullets. It just trimmed my hair on the right side
of my head while sniping at the Germans. It's some sport.
I certainly play with ammunition especially when I get
into the game. We were in the firing line all right.
I could smell my hair burning. First twelve hours
I did not have time to eat – too fond of sniping.

– Francis Pegahmagabow, *Toronto Star*, Tuesday, 23 March 1915

(Early days
boys
Early days)

Pen in hand Francis signs on,
a pat on the shoulder,
and he is like any other man.
To training camp off he goes,
but what they don't know
is he can shoot a hopping rabbit
a good quarter-mile away.

OFFICER   So you want to be in the Northern Pioneer
regiment. Odd
for an Indian,
but let's get on with it then:
one, two, three,
one, two, three, march!
Now stand over there
and let's see
what you can do.
Look down the way,
see those target sheets.
Now load,
and shoot.

It's during target practice that the officers
take note. They don't say anything
but look on in surprise.
His great-grandfather a warrior chief in 1812,
must be the fighting instinct
in the blood.
Otherwise
how to account
for such an eye?

A KISS OF TRANSLATION

What the ancients called a ~~smart, shrewd, resourceful, astute, ingenious~~, gifted fighter is one who not only wins
but excels in winning with ease.

– Sun Tzu, *The Art of War,* 5th century BCE

A MOST PERNICIOUS THING

By about 1400, possibly in Genoa, a firearm which permitted one man
to aim, load, and fire was developed. In its many stages of evolution,
this firearm is referred to as the "matchlock." . . . The matchlock
evolved slowly

(Serpentine Cock Set
Flint ignition Frizzen spark
Cap percussion Nipple detonation
Pan urgency Butt Plate recoil
Patch Box ordinance nucleus Breech
envisioned Ramrod dystopia
à la Barrel blaze Muzzle disruption
dimension Stock & Lock authoritative
Plate prediction Key conquest
Rear Sight innovative
To future Front Sight intervention
commerce Wedge precision
release Ball hunger
Hammer
Trigger)

from 1450 to 1600. The most glaring fault of the matchlock
was that a lighted match had to be carried at all times.
It was not uncommon for arquebusiers to be caught without matches lit,
rendering their weapons useless. By 1600, settlement
in the New World by the Spanish, French, English, Dutch, and Swedes
had begun. Hostilities involving indigenous populations
began almost immediately.
Armour remained in fashion for some time.

– Brian J. Given, *A Most Pernicious Thing: Gun Trading and Native Warfare
in the Early Contact Period,* 1994

Moved to Valcartier training camp
there's a surfeit of volunteers
in these early recruiting days,
and hundreds
are sent home.
A directive has come down
forbidding Indians to fight,
but that's all right,
Lieutenant-Colonel F.W. Hill
is tough as nails,
and he looks for the hammer
where he can find it.

Lt.Col. F.W. HILL   Peggy, you're one of us!
You'll stay and join the fight overseas.

FRANCIS   They call me one of them,
but I remember
the old Medicine Man
near Thunder Bay.
I welcomed his medicine gift
because I sensed
it contained a kind of power,
few today acknowledge,
or truly understand.

A WORD FROM THE NARRATOR'S NARRATOR

I know what you are thinking

The Narrator knows everything

Hand of God Sleight of Hand

Same thing depending on

Our Father Who Art dealing the hand

YEARS LATER FRANCIS TELLS THE ANTHROPOLOGIST DIAMOND JENNESS OF HIS ENCOUNTER WITH POWER

When I was at Rossport, on Lake Superior, in 1914, some of us landed
from our vessel to gather blueberries near an Ojibwa camp. An old Indian
recognized me, and gave me a tiny medicine-bag to protect me, saying that
I would shortly go into great danger. The bag was of skin, tightly bound
with a leather thong. Sometimes it seemed to be as hard as rock,
at other times it appeared to contain nothing.
What really was inside it I do not know.
I wore it in the trenches, but lost it when I was wounded
and taken to a hospital.

– Diamond Jenness, *The Ojibwa Indians of Parry Island*, 1935

SCENE TWO: THE WARRIOR – HEREIN FRANCIS FINDS HIMSELF IN THE WAR THAT WILL END WAR WHILE HIS GUARDIAN SPIRIT LOOKS ON

Francis in the Trenches – His Manido Speaks.

DEER SPIRIT In the trenches, in the muck
in the stench of death
the young soldiers
come to believe
in something greater
than what they see
greater than themselves
greater than cannon and shell
in all they witness
in their living hell.

Ordered to continue
to the last man
they want nothing more
than to understand.
Down on their knees
or standing tall
they look to the sky
the universe
so large
and they so small.

THE WARRIORS

Death's chief victims in war are young men or
youths who . . . must take leave of their lives
under conditions of exposure, away from home, without
the possibility of the dignity and ceremony that help
to moderate death's shocking character. The difference is
not only between dying and getting killed. It is much more
the difference between dying by disease or accident
among people who know and cherish you
and having your life cut off.

– J. Glenn Gray, *The Warriors*, 1959

POETRY TO SOOTHE YOUR SOUL

Look up
Look down
(Sooner or later it's fire and sorrow banging at your door
more war deplore can't ignore)
Too little too late you're shrapnelled on the ground
same roar without a sound

Get thee a rhyming dictionary and substitute as you like:
pound
hound (as in hell)
round (as in bomb)
drowned (as in mud or fear)
Be as creative as you like: bound (as in to this hellhole
or duty or job or just plain tied up)
confound (are you confounded?)
dumbfound (are you dumb?
war will do that)
~~wound~~
merry-go-round!
Around and around we go

The 1st Battalion arrives in Europe
and marches steadfast
into Belgium,
arrives at a spot of ground
called Ypres
still not claimed by the Germans.
But to their horror
the Canadians find
they are totally unprepared
for the war,
none have experienced anything
like this ever before:
a foot of sewer water
in the trenches
surrounded by razor-sharp
barbed wire fences,
a steady barrage of artillery fire
dropping upon the men,
the shells disinter the bodies
then bury them again,
sniper bullets zinging
while ghostly flares
illumine the dead,
six thousand cylinders of gas
released in the air,
soldiers vomiting
turning green
running scared

a stalemate of armies
dug in like dung beetles
fatly fed
on a daily ration of blood meal.

A HIT HOME RUN DRONE ON

Rule #1: Evade: Answer a question with a question.

Rule #2: Not too much, don't run, or it becomes treason.

Rule #3: All oiled up we march with righteousness on our side of the gun.

Rule #4: Memorize the proper language, without it everything falls apart.

Military Operation Military Mining Skirmish Shoot and Scoot
Scorched Earth Circumvallation Information Management
Rout Pincer Manoeuvre Guerrilla Tactics Extraction Point Friendly
Fire Low-Level Bombing Artillery Barrage Breach

Check your language.

Language grown from language into more language.
Clandestine Covert Surreptitious Deceitful Cunning.
Add to this language a few s/words like
Casualty Grief Maimed Mad Sad Lad
(meaning still-wet-behind-the-y/ears
good for cannon fodder).

Build your language.

Come up with your own
(though don't intentionally muddy the water
trying too hard to showdown):
neutralized ~~fucking~~ live resource
~~fucking~~ cherry bombed hospital
blood infusion ~~fucking~~ cocktail
limited ~~fucking~~ engagement ring
(whatever ~~the fuck~~ that means).

Drone on

OFFICER   Stand-to, wait for the whistle.
               Bayonets fixed,
               we're going over the top,
               shoulder to shoulder.

FRANCIS   We run straight into a storm
               of machine gun bullets.

               No turning back.

               We bend into it like it's hail.
               Then the mortar begins,
               shrapnel razing the ground.
               Every second man
               in the 1st and 4th Divisions goes down.

               How can you trust
               an officer after that?

OFFICER   Chin up, boys, we'll get them next time.

FRANCIS   Thompson, Hall and Chapelle too,
               I watch them die
               and learn quick enough,
               there's little I can do.
               Boys, spilling out their guts,
               calling for their mothers –

- cliché I admit
you've heard it a thousand times
though any way you cut it you can't escape it
grown men-boys crying to crawl back
into the womb

A VERY SHORT NOTE
ON BEING INDIAN IN CANADA

To stay alive
To vote or
Not
That is
To be Indian

OFFICER	The only way to win this war is to fight fire with fire. I call for snipers to go out at night and gather information on the enemy. Claim the Hun by speed or stealth, bullet or knife, the work needs to be done.
FRANCIS	He calls it work, but I've known work since I was a child. I know hunting too. This he orders is something else.
OFFICER	Peggy, it's up to you.
FRANCIS	Yes, Sir!

Number	649377
Surname	SPANIEL
Christian Name	John
Units	52nd Bn Can In
Theatre of War	France
Rank	Pte
Date of Service	29-11-16
Remarks	
Latest Address	Biscotasing
Roll No.	Can: Orthopedic Christie St. Toronto ont
Page 11963.	
200m-2-21.M.	

A NOTE ON UNCLE JOHN

I think of this son of Sahquakesgick who joined up after his brother Joe was killed in 1915. John later wounded in Mons, France, and sent to the Christie Street Hospital in Toronto to recover with other veterans. War wrecks trying to heal from blindness, amputation, madness. Or the wretched of the war wasting away from tuberculosis. The convalescing soldiers, Uncle John among them, spending May to October lying on metal cots on the hospital's rooftop to get the maximum exposure to the sun. They came to be called Sun-Worshippers. Which makes me think of a warm summer day lounging on the beach.

His compatriots called John the clichéd name Big Chief. Considering what the men went through together, I like to think it was a name that signified friendship and even respect – they had depended on their Indian sharpshooters. Little did they know that John came from a family of chiefs, grandfather, father, uncles, all chiefs of the Spanish River – Sagamok Anishnawbek – First Nation. All signatories to treaty. Little did they know that over one hundred years later he would find his way into this book.

A SHORT NOTE ON BROTHER JOE LOST AMONG THE ROWS AND ROWS OF WHITE CROSSES*

Reference Code:	File - C 273-1-0-17-7
Title:	[Joe Espaniel from Benny on the Canadian Pacific Railroad line between Sudbury and Chapleau, in his Canadian Expeditionary Force uniform. He was killed overseas]
Date of Creation:	[ca. 1915]

Then it's April, springtime,
a time of flowers
and new growth,
but it's 1916,
and the number of dead float in the air
like tiny droplets of dew.
How do you make sense of it?
133,000 French,
100,000 British,
including Canadians,
120,000 Germans, and on and on,
until the little drops of dew
become an ocean
and mean little or nothing,
unless it's someone you knew.

OFFICER   A fine job done.
               I'm putting you up for a commendation.
               But why are you such a loner?

FRANCIS   I go out with others at first.
               I turn to my partner
               but he only has half a head,
               and I come back alone
               and swear:
               no spotter for me
               from that point on.

CONTEXTUAL INTERLUDE

Dear Armand:

I hope this message finds you well amidst these troubling times in Canada and around the world. I want to share a moving story about Rana,* a brave mother from Sudan. While she was shopping at a local market, violence suddenly broke out. Fearing for her safety, Rana swiftly fled the chaos, desperate to get home to her children.

Realizing their home was no longer safe, Rana made the difficult decision to escape with her family. With immense determination, she gathered her children and embarked on a harrowing journey to seek refuge. Eventually, they reached a Save the Children centre supporting displaced families like hers.

– A letter from Save the Children, 9 June 2023

WE ARE "CHILDREN, NOT SOLDIERS"

In 2014, with UNICEF, the Special Representative launched the campaign "Children, Not Soldiers" to bring about a global consensus that child soldiers should not be used in conflict. The campaign was designed to generate momentum, political will and international support to turn the page once and for all on the recruitment of children by national security forces in conflict situations.

– United Nations, Office of the Special Representative of the Secretary-General for Children and Armed Conflict

OFFICER   I see a few of the men behaving like you
               and putting down tobacco.
               This is a Christian war by George!
               What are these things
               you do?

FRANCIS   Look around, the constant bombing
               has turned the land
               into a graveyard,
               skeleton trees marking the dead.
               I take a piece of one of the branches
               put it in my month
               and become the grey earth.
               My medicine is strong
               and I feel invisible
               invincible.

HOW MANY TIMES IS WAR MENTIONED IN THE BIBLE?

OneTwoThreeFourFiveSixSevenEightNineTenTwentyThirtyTimes?
Clearly God Is a Busy Man

Tonight we will sit in our assigned seats
and when the curtain
goes up on the side of war
we will war on.

Let us begin with Genesis and run to Exodus,
if that is your persuasion
and go from there.

The Lord is a warrior. Authorized King James Version, Exodus 15:3.

Or to put it another way to even the playing field.

The Lord is a man of war. Revised Standard Version, Catholic edition,
Exodus 15:3.

A righteous act bleeding the good book
(not your persuasion? Look,
we drag our weapons behind us like a tail).

A NEWS FLASH, 8 OCTOBER 2023

Today the manuscript, and the Middle East explodes
again. Hamas attacks Israel and turns a music concert
into a field of slaughter. Israel retaliates.
Sends in its fighter aircraft and pounds Gaza
into the ground. ~~Hundreds~~
Thousands[1] dead and counting.
Tit-for-tat and rat-a-tat-tat go the guns.
Boom-boom-boom go the bombs.
So it goes
humankind does what it does ~~best~~.

1   According to the Al Jazeera news network, as of Remembrance Day, November 11, 2023, 4,500 children have been killed in the war, including the bombing of the Al-Nasr Children's Hospital in Gaza City. On and on it goes. At the time of going to print, according to Save the Children, the number of children killed had risen to 13,800 with more that 12,000 injured.

OFFICER	You're a good soldier, Pegahmagabow, but you're a rather big swell!
FRANCIS	The Military Medal, and I am treated like a new recruit.
OFFICER	As your new commanding officer, I simply can't believe your report.
FRANCIS	When you get killed or captured, you'll believe it.
OFFICER	I could have you arrested for that.
FRANCIS	I was in the trenches before you even signed on.
OFFICER	You're out of line.
FRANCIS	Maybe yes, maybe no. But what I do know is my job is to scout and snipe and take the enemy out, and I'm the best at what I do. With my Ross rifle and scope I count over three hundred targets I see in the crosshairs flesh and blood, just like me and you.

PRIVATE FRANCIS PEGAHMAGABOW
APPOINTED LANCE CORPORAL

First commendation

Lance-Corporal Francis Pegahmagabow, one of the first Canadians
to earn the Military Medal.

Military Medal Citation, *London Gazette*, No. 29608, 3 June 1916
For continuous service as a messenger from February 14th, 1915,
to February 1916. He carried messages with great bravery and success
during the whole of the actions at Ypres, Festubert and Givenchy.
In all his work he has consistently shown a disregard
for danger and his faithfulness to duty is highly commendable.

Second commendation

The Military Medal Bar citation, *London Gazette*, No. 30573,
13 March 1918. At Passchendaele Nov. 6th/7th, 1917, this NCO
[non-commissioned officer] did excellent work. Before and after the attack
he kept in touch with the flanks. Advising the units he had seen,
this information proving the success of the attack and saving
valuable time in consolidating. He also guided the relief to its proper
place after it had become mixed up.

– Canadian War Museum

CONTEXTUAL NOTE ON COMMENDATIONS

It was said that no one could understand war without first setting foot
in a military hospital. The images of human bodies torn apart
or eaten alive by infection imprinted themselves on
the medical service personnel.

– Tim Cook, *Lifesavers and Body Snatchers*, 2022

(Impossible to describe the smell
you cannot
smell
unless you were there
a smell
you could never
wash away –
take to your own grave.)

The war takes its toll
like a disease, a contagion
from which nobody is immune
leaving both solders
and countries in ruins.
Another year, one hundred-pound shells,
65,000 tonnes fired at Passchendaele.
Stalemate on both sides,
everybody fails.
November 1917,
the Canadians finally take it.
Total losses on the British side
some 245,000 men,
not counting the French and the Germans.

And then Peggy gets shot in the leg
and sent to England
to recuperate.

A WORD FROM OUR SPONSOR WHO STANDS OUTSIDE THE ACTION AND SEES ALL – A GOD BUT NOT A GOD BECAUSE GOOD GOD

Here's the thing, Canada. I write this in the comfort of my home
in the clouds, for which I am grateful, and yet
I cannot help but ask how many people are fleeing war
at this very moment. I glance outside and see a neighbour
with white wings. She is walking her little Scottie
dressed in its cozy plaid blanket. A heavenly scene
if there ever was one. And yet
press a button, and you can see the displaced
dragging their bodies along
with their few salvaged possessions,
somewhere, everywhere. Think about it.

I google the UN Refugee Agency. An unprecedented one hundred
million around the world have been forced to flee their homes.
Among them 27.1 million refugees, 41 percent
under the age of eighteen. There are also millions
of stateless people denied
a nationality and lack access to basic rights
such as education, healthcare, employment and
freedom of movement. Think about it.

Contemporary facts for the displaced, but, O Canada,
your country like all settler states is a country of refugees
fleeing war in all its amputated manifestations.
Beginning with the French, English, Scottish, Irish . . .
all marching onward into today.
(At a fallout glance: Rwanda, Yemen, Libya, Afghanistan,
Ethiopia, Sudan, Ukraine, Palestine __ , __ fill in
the blanks.) Facts and figures, meaningless
after a few generations when
the refugee-immigrant forgets
and feels almost Indigenous, but not quite
– always the angry itch – and points a finger
at those damn OTHERS. Think about it.

SCENE THREE: WOUNDED – HEREIN FRANCIS SUFFERS THE FATE OF MILLIONS AND BECOMES ANOTHER CASUALTY

FRANCIS   When they ask me about getting wounded
I tell them I lost my faith.
It's difficult to keep it
in a place like this.
With it went the tiny medicine bag
given to me
by the old Shaman.
Sometimes it felt hard as rock,
at other times
like it contained nothing.

(THE NARRATOR'S NARRATOR INTERRUPTS
        AND REVEALS HIMSELF TO SET THE RECORD STRAIGHT)

As soon as he's physically able
he's back on the front
and in the thick of it.

But he's not the same,
not as stable they say,
and he's sent to Lord Derby War Hospital
where they look for what's wrong
but they know all along.
The average life
in the trenches
is six months.

He's been dug in
for nearly four years.

A NOTE ON WHAT IS GOING ON AT THE HOME FRONT

I was raised in a northern town that had a residential school.
The original Chapleau St. John's Anglican Residential School ran
from 1907 to 1919, and a second, bigger school to accommodate
more children ran from 1920 to 1948. An unmarked graveyard
consisting of forty-two graves was discovered near the second
school between the road and railway tracks leading into the town.
To think the children in these schools were dying at unprecedented
rates while their fathers were off fighting for the country.

RESTING II

See the hidden graves between the trees,
the unmarked ones,
the ones that will be forever nameless,
the children are resting. Resting?
As if each child were tucked in
with a lullaby, a teddy bear,
a goodnight kiss.

It isn't true. Where do the lies come from?
They are not resting.
Though we do what we can for them,
pray, sing, put down tobacco,
burn sweetgrass and sage,
watch little hearts of smoke curling up towards the sky.

Listen, they are below our feet.
Can you hear them?
Their tiny bones are turning as I speak,
turning to dust
turning to soil
turning to plants and animals,
in turn turning.

Look there, carefully, over by that mound
barely noticeable under the damp leaves.
You can see their thin arms
tendrils of green
reaching
twisting
pushing
up through the earth.

[W]hen the killing starts, whether it's on the plains of Montana or in the deserts of Iraq, everyone ends up covered with blood.

– Thomas King, *The Inconvenient Indian*, 2012

HOMEFRONT ACT
ENDAANG EN'KAMGAK

SCENE ONE: A RETURNED HERO – HEREIN FRANCIS RETURNS HOME AND STRUGGLES WITHOUT SUPPORT

DEER SPIRIT   What about those who no one sees
no shattered bones
or missing limbs
a wound whose roots go deeper
than the tallest
majestic tree.

Let us mourn
for the ones who died
were resurrected
and returned
abandoned
and forgotten
in a country
they no longer recognized.

THEY CALL IT SHELL SHOCK²

As a **new medical phenomenon**, it took **time** for **shell shock** to be
recognized and **understood** by the medical profession.

What we felt: we'd **rather lose a leg**, be wounded, anything, but
to have shell shock. That'd come out and their fingers would be waving
like tissue paper. Oh they were shaking all the time and wild looking,
that type. The strain of **continual bombardment** – not just one bomb**,**
continual bombardment
all the time
pounding and **pounding continually** away.

(The veteran dreams he is dying
or he is watching
the dying
die.

Carrying death is hard work.)

That's what people don't understand.
One of my friends who went over there, when he came back
after the war, he shut himself up in his home
and wouldn't come out at all. He finished up in a **lunatic asylum**
and **died** only a year or two after the war.

There are people that say there's **no such thing** as shell shock.
They should have been there.

– Imperial War Museum, London, UK

2   "The term 'shell-shock' should be reserved for the condition which follows exposure to the
forces generated by the explosion of powerful shells in the absence of any visible injury to the
head or spine." – Arthur F. Hurst, Royal Victoria Hospital, Netley (where Francis was treated),
"Shell-Shock, Chapter IV," *Medical Diseases of the War*, second edition, 1918.

April 1919, and Francis Pegahmagabow
returns a hero.
He has sniped 378 of the enemy,
and has virtually lasted
the duration of the war.

The Military Medal
and two bars
directly from the Prince of Wales,
he is far from a regular soldier
sliding unnoticed into the ranks
of civilian life.

He moves back to the island of Wasauksing
determined to pick up
where he left off.
He soon marries
and children are born.

Life has never been better,
and yet for him there is still the storm
rising on great
wings.

FRANCIS   I brush off my uniform
and take up arms
and patrol the reserve
roads at night.
I'm determined to protect my wife
and children.
The neighbours open their curtains
and wonder what I'm doing.
How do I explain
what I still see –
magnified just for me.

MILITARY MEDAL SECOND BAR CITATION

The 1st Battalion relieved the 3rd Division in the line on 16 August 1918.
In their next action, Francis Pegahmagabow earned his second bar
to the Military Medal in the Battle of the Scarpe. During the operations of
August 30, 1918, at Orix Trench, near Upton Wood, when his company
were almost out of ammunition and in danger of being surrounded,
this NCO went over the top under heavy MG [machine gun] and rifle fire
and brought back sufficient ammunition to enable the post to carry on
and assist in repulsing heavy enemy counter-attacks.

– The 1st Division Order No. 5465 of 3 October 1918,
Canadian War Museum

A NOTE ON NORMALIZING WAR OR NOT THE
KIND OF PARTY YOU WANT TO ATTEND

Storming Party of Snipers

The actual storming party consisted of thirteen men. We crept up
until were within 20 yards of the enemy's trench, our bayonets
being fixed as we crept up, and when the order was given to charge
we leapt right into the German trench with but few casualties
so far as I know. Then followed the storming party
with picks, shovel and bombs. The German trench
was partly evacuated before they got in, but those who remained
were bayoneted. Three prisoners were taken in the retiring
from the trench in accordance with orders, two of the prisoners were
killed by their own maxims. The Germans made a counterattack
and there were probably altogether 60 casualties
among the Princess Patricias.

– *Toronto Star*, Tuesday, 23 March 1915

REPORTER   Mr. Pegahmagabow,
             is it true what they're saying? Over three hundred sniped!
             How is it possible?

FRANCIS   I had help.

REPORTER   What do you mean?

FRANCIS   There's always help if we believe.
             One night we were overtaken
             not by guns
             but by a terrific thunderstorm.
             I felt the air flap around my face
             and I was shaken
             by the wings of a mighty bird.
             I knew at that instant
             I was in the midst
             of what we call Biidweyaangwe,
             the coming sound of a thunderbird's wings.

REPORTER   Well, you don't say.

A SHORT EUPHEMISM ALERT

To snipe (verb), from to shoot snipes, a kind of bird; also to shoot
at a target or to shoot at an individual and to put yourself in danger,
as in the risk of getting shot yourself, and maimed as in amputated,
or killed, as in death, dead, died (in action, yet another euphemism).

A NOTE ON BIIDWEYAANGWE

Previously he had not believed the story of a thunderbird,
but on this occasion at least
it seemed to him that it must be true.

– Diamond Jenness, *The Ojibwa Indians of Parry Island*, 1935

ON THE INEXPLICABLE

Some months after she died, he had a birthday.
It was a bright winter morning, and he opened
the back door wondering what the day would bring.
There on the fence was a large hawk, sitting
as though it had been waiting for him to come out.
He froze momentarily watching it eyeing him
and then he dashed through the snow towards it.
He saw it flit downwards and figured it could not
have gone far, but when he reached the spot
it was gone. He searched the ground,
surveyed the sky. There was
absolutely no trace of it.

Raise your left hand, your heart hand, if
something like this has happened to you.

SCENE TWO: THE ACTIVIST – HEREIN FRANCIS REALIZES THAT HE MUST DO SOMETHING TO CHANGE THE WAY CANADA TREATS HIS PEOPLE

The first thing Francis realizes
is the gulf between cultures
is as wide as the Great Lakes.
Some are quick to comment
that his record must be fake,
but even more pressing
is the lack of respect
a primitive people, they say,
who cannot manage their own affairs.

Francis Meets an Agent of the Indian Department.

FRANCIS   I'd like a loan to buy a cow from old Mrs. Keeshig.

AGENT   A waste of money.

FRANCIS   I can sell the extra milk.

AGENT   Someone in need will knock on your door. And there it goes.

FRANCIS   A cow will give my family a head start.

AGENT   I can get you a job fixing roads, cutting railway ties.

FRANCIS   My lungs suffer from the war.

AGENT   Well then, I'll see what I can do. Time's up, I'll get back to you.

RETURNING HOME TO THE RESERVE

Francis says that away from family his comrades-in-arms become
his family, and that's who he's fighting for. When the shit's flying,
prejudice falls away quickly, at least for a while. Later
he will be shocked and dismayed and finally angry
at the treatment he receives at the war's end. The Indian Agent
who held the rank of a lowly private suddenly has power
over Francis, a corporal, and uses it to seek revenge.

(Bet your bottom dollar this is happening across the country.)

A NOTE ON TREATY BENEFITS

Treaty benefits in Canada go something like this.
Say you have a toothache and you don't have any private
insurance or money. You call up the health line
for the Department of Indigenous [read Indian] Affairs.
You need their approval
before the dentist will do the work
so he can get reimbursed. The phone rings
and rings and rings. An hour later
someone answers. You explain the situation,
and they tell you that they need to see X-rays before
they can approve the work. But the dentist won't do
the X-rays without the department's approval.
They got you. Classic Catch-22.
Bad tooth. Too bad.

A loan to buy a cow
a team of horses, a farm
under the Soldier Settlement Act,
the Indian Agent scoffs
and scorns,
and won't support Francis's application.
He tells the government
he's too much of a risk,
too temperamental,
not right in the head,
just because the man's a veteran,
doesn't mean he should expect compensation.
Turned away again and again,
even with the Band's support,
Francis wonders
what his sacrifice was all about.

FRANCIS   Equality
in the trenches in a time of need,
but now I'm back to the end of the line
with barely enough to feed my family.

RECONCILIATION IS RESTITUTION

Driving through cottage country, a necklace of turquoise lakes
on a sunny afternoon, I've come to visit my relatives
and I wave as I pass other Anishnaabek families.

Some are lounging on their deck looking out
to where kayaks and canoes dot the water, some
are repairing their own canoes
or making them.

My window is rolled down and I catch the soft lull of
our language on my tongue. There are children playing,
grandparents watching over them, parents chatting
nearby under a canopy of leafy trees.

The old memories of lies, broken treaties, dispersal,
isolation, clapboard houses, dusty roads, concrete ghettos,
boarded windows, black mould, undrinkable water

Endless unemployment, boredom in rock and swamp,
in mined, dammed, clear-cut, and bulldozed landscapes,
residential schools, foster care, prison, rape, murder, suicide,
alcohol, drugs, the misery of invasion,
loss, loss, loss, loss, loss, loss, loss, loss, loss, loss, loss.

It is all history now.
Something we tell our children
so they won't forget
while trying not to scare them.

FOOTNOTE TO THE HISTORY OF CANADA

Separated from their families the Children were crushed by loneliness.

– Truth and Reconciliation Commission, *Interim Report*, 2012

(FOOTNOTE REDUX: Count your blessings you or your children
did not end up in one of those *special* schools,
no fault of your own.)

A time when everything Indian
is banned and shunned,
his people are subject to the whim
of the Indian department
which hands out Band payments
like a child's allowance.

At one time owning the whole Parry Sound region and more.
Waaseyaakosing, "the place that shines brightly
in the reflection of sacred light,"
and then deceived.

Even their tiny island home
is taken without compensation.
J.R. Booth, king of the Ottawa Valley lumber barons,
with influential government connections,
gets hundreds of acres
for his Atlantic Railway depot.
His last request: burn his papers,
cover his tracks.

ON HEARING WORDS ON A CASSETTE TAPE

The other day I found a box full of old cassette recordings. Some of them
had labels indicating what was recorded. Most didn't. I took one that didn't
and slipped it into my mother's old player, salvaged
before it went to the dump. It took a moment
for the machine to warm up and the reels to pick up speed. Finally
a voice at the other end of time went from a bluuuur to a young woman
saying something about organizing. It was a political gathering.

The recording was poor, it sounded like the speaker was at the end
of a long hallway. I had to listen hard. Whoever made it clearly didn't know
what they were doing. She seemed to be talking personally about her own
hard life and the lives of women she knew.
Then it struck me who made the recording. I did.
I had been asked to be the secretary for a meeting
of the Native Women's Association of Canada.
I suppose someone didn't show up and someone else figured
I could do it. After all, I was a student at the university and
there were not very many of us in those days.
I must have taken the tape back to my apartment to transcribe it
and then thrown it into the box.

The voices were passionately advocating for change in the lives
of Indigenous women. I figured it had to be the early '80s. Heady times.
A time when you could count the number of Indigenous organizations in
Ottawa on your hands. I thought back to the protest
for NATO Out of Nitassinan, the Constitution Express,
the blockade at Couchiching I took part in. And here
I was all those years later sitting in a basement among boxes listening
to some badly recorded words which today are nothing less
than a small flame
cupped in a hand
against a bitter wind. A flame we still hold
because without it we would freeze.
And so I pass it to you.
Take this flame now.
Take this flame.

Francis Realizes Straight Away Something Must Be Done. He Addresses the Indian Agent.

FRANCIS   The Canadian National Lumber and Tie Company
           is cutting all the valuable timber on the Reserve
           and not giving us anything.
           We want it stopped.

AGENT   The Indian Department would have to approve it.

FRANCIS   That's why I'm here.

AGENT   Duly noted.

FRANCIS   And our beautiful Sandy Island?
           Shkodeng-mnis,
           the place where the spirits live.
           It was never in the treaty.
           White people are building summer homes there.

AGENT   I'll see what I can do. Time's up, I'll get back to you.

FRANCIS PEGAHMAGABOW DOES THE UNTHINKABLE AND OBJECTS

I have seen Indians with nothing to eat in their place.
Sam Devlin [the Indian Agent] just laughs at them saying
"What do you think, I am Santa Claus?"
He gives rations only to the ones he likes, and he will not speak a word
to get work for an Indian. He gives us no protection.
We go to tell him the white people are trespassing on our reserve and
he just laughs at us. He would say: "Why not shoot them with an arrow?"
He is a man who naturally hates an Indian.

– Francis Pegahmagabow, letter, 22 January 1941

A SHORT INTERLUDE #2

An Indian greets a white guy and says, Aunii, Hello.
The white guy is surprised and says,
I thought you Indians said How.
We know how, replies the Indian.
We just want a chance.

O CANADA OUR HOME ON NATIVE LAND

Something Indigenous people sing
aloud
or under their breath
on Canada Day

DEER SPIRIT   Francis prays to the Great Spirit.
              Beseeches the Manidos for intervention.
              Attends the Catholic mass devoutly.
              Prays to Jesus Christ
              who sent a nun to care for him
              when he thought he would lose his leg.

              And still the iron fist of the Indian Department beats down.
              Francis is desperate for change
              and runs for Chief.
              But the government calls the shots,
              and there's not a lot the Band can do,
              except write letters
              and pass council resolutions,
              and then Francis comes up with a solution.

              He starts organizing politically
              and joins the newly formed
              Brotherhood of Canadian Indians,
              and helps establish
              the National Indian Government.

WHEREIN A MEDICINE DREAM COMES
FROM AN UNLIKELY SOURCE

After I returned from the war I was ill and unable to do a hard day's work.
One night I dreamed that Jesus approached me, clothed in a loincloth and
with bleeding wounds as He appears in pictures. I threw myself at his feet
and asked for a blessing. Then I awoke and told my friends that Jesus
had blessed me and was restoring my health. I recovered my health
and I am now as strong as ever.

– Francis Pegahmagabow to Diamond Jenness,
The Ojibwa Indians of Parry Island, 1935

A NOTE FROM THE STREET

Earlier today I had a few errands
to do downtown
and flew over the fallen –
homeless shell-shocked
battle-scarred
life imploded strect crippled
brother, sister, daughter, son –
pressed hard into their concrete bed.
From my vantage point I could see
they were begging our survival.
As our flock veered away in another direction
I swooped in and dropped a few dollars
which they eagerly grabbed and ate.

Francis Addresses the Indian Agent.

FRANCIS   We want our rights.

AGENT   Order under the British flag above all.

FRANCIS   Then we'll bypass Indian Affairs and go directly to King George.

AGENT   I'll remove you as Chief.

FRANCIS   For what reason?

AGENT   Incompetence. You're of no value to me or the Band.

FRANCIS   I'll hire a lawyer.

AGENT   Lawyers cost money.

FRANCIS   I'll raise the money.

AGENT   It's against the law.

FRANCIS   I'll fight.

AGENT   Listen, the majority want things to stay the way they are.

FRANCIS   Because the government holds back Band payments if we don't stay quiet.

AGENT   Time's up. Time to go.

INDIANS LAUNCH PROTEST AT SECRET COUNCIL SESSION

A Protest against the blocking of treaty rights . . . Canada's 150,000 Indians are practically destitute. They are dependent on the Indian Affairs Branch in Ottawa, composed of whites. Indians are not receiving proper education. What schools there are do not fit the Indian to take his proper place in his own society, and certainly not in the society of white men.

— Francis Pegahmagabow, *Sudbury Daily Star*, 15 October 1946

In October 1946 shortly after returning from the first parliament of the National Indian Government in Detroit, Francis Pegahmagabow attended a secret meeting in Biscotasing, northern Ontario, to discuss the growing problem [of restrictions on fishing and hunting rights].

— Adrian Hayes, *Pegahmagabow: Life-Long Warrior*, 2009

It appears they chose Biscotasing (or Bisco as we still call the village) in remote northern Ontario because up there they could get away from the prying eye of the Indian Agent. Uncle John lived in the area at the time and I am left wondering if he and Francis met. I like to think they would have been kindred spirits. Though in different regiments during the war they would have experienced the same horrors on the battlefield and later the same hardships trying to survive in colonial Canada.

John moose hunting, posing with his mother, Sarah, and sister Margaret

SCENE THREE: THE GOOD FIGHT – HEREIN FRANCIS MOVES TO THE SPIRIT LEVEL

Then it is over.
Francis is voted out of office.
He joins the peacetime militia
and feels the old camaraderie again,
his medals pinned to his chest.
Equality and fraternity
in the khaki uniform.
He is greeted as one of the best.
For a while he's an ambassador
for the military.
In procession he stops to comfort a mother
who has lost two sons in the war.

THE NARRATOR'S NARRATOR HAS A ~~LAST~~ WORD

Last Wrong World Winning

It got to a point that everywhere I turned
pointed me in the ~~wrong~~ direction
and I soon found myself directionless,
embarrassment, or was it earnestness,
bunched around my ankles.
At the national there was a daughter fighting
the government to exhume her murdered
mother from a trash heap.[1] Another inquiry with no teeth.[2]
(So) I watched the helpless ~~world~~ watch helplessly
watching it play out again and again in real time.
At the international I learned by rote the unmessage,
steady as she goes, a nation's military is a crucial asset.
The military enforces domestic and foreign policies
and protects its citizens. There could be no denying it.
(So) in response I memorized in order
the top ten ~~winning~~ countries with the highest military
expenditures for the year of our Lord 2022 – USA, $811.6B; China, $298B;
India $81B; Saudi Arabia, $73B; Russia, $72B; United Kingdom, $70B;
Germany, $57.8B; France, $57B; Japan, $53B; South Korea, $49.6B"[3]
– (as) I ordered a western for lunch, heavy on the hope,
and told myself that a billion is not
what it used to be (couldn't be).

1   Steve Lambert, "Blockade Continues at Winnipeg Landfill as Protesters Demand Search for Missing Women," *Toronto Star*, July 10, 2023, www.thestar.com/politics/blockade-continues-at-winnipeg-landfill-as-protesters-demand-search-for-missing-women/article_9fe31542-e898-5919-aabc-531f3fe0a413.html.

2   Angela Johnston and Karen Pauls, "No Stone Left Unturned: MMIWG Families Skeptical Police Will Change," CBC News, June 3, 2019, www.cbc.ca/news/canada/manitoba/no-stone-left-unturned-mmiwg-families-skeptical-police-will-change-1.5160911; Rosemary Barton, "Over 20 Years Ago, We Had a Plan to Repair the Crown-Indigenous Relationship. What Happened?," February 28, 2020, www.cbc.ca/news/politics/royal-commission-indigenous-crown-1.5478890; Manuela Vega, "6 Years after TRC Report, Canada Is Failing to 'Rectify Ongoing Harms' against Indigenous Communities, New Report Charges," March 1, 2022, www.thestar.com/news/canada/6-years-after-trc-report-canada-is-failing-to-rectify-ongoing-harms-against-indigenous-communities/article_03739d6f-5c88-5e15-98ce-45ea79ad826f.html.

3   "Military Spending by Country 2024," World Population Review, 2024, worldpopulationreview.com/country-rankings/military-spending-by-country.

DEER SPIRIT   Though we think we know
              what really matters
              we live in the world of souls
              and shadows.
              Intervention
              comes when we least expect it.
              Around us human
              and spirit
              the known
              and the unknown.
              A snap of a finger
              and we are in their midst.

CONSIDERING A SACRED SONG

That's the way, isn't it

We are told

And should never forget

To realize we are never alone

Our ancestors the ones who foresaw us

As we see them

Are always with us

And this love

Is like a great wind

That holds us up when we least expect it

And carries us

Like children

Across the sky

Francis's militia work, too, comes to an end.
And with support from the military
Francis is finally
given a disability pension.
But still under the yoke of Indian Affairs
no Veteran benefits for him.
Always one step behind,
or one step ahead,
the Indian Department still calls the shots,
continues to put up roadblocks
to curtail treaty rights,
human rights.

For Francis, it has always been
the good fight.

Francis Is Weary and Pensive. His Life Is Coming to an End.

FRANCIS　　　I like to spend my time with my family now.
I take my children to Church,
and we sing the old hymns.
I also teach them what's important,
our language
and our ceremonies,
the land,
the things we need to take care of.
People still come asking for help.
I do what I can.
And then there are those who offer help.

It is good to have faith.

The language, culture, and stories of the Nishnaabeg were a natural part of community life for Francis Pegahmagabow. He would be among the last to grow up with the older generation.

What Francis could not have known was that English would almost exclusively dominate the lives of the people. This almost total loss of language, Duncan [Francis's son] once commented to me, would have hurt him more than any injury sustained in the Great War.

– Brian McInnis, Aanikobijigan, great-grandson of Francis Pegahmagabow

Francis Pegahmagabow in Ottawa for a conference of the National Indian Government, 1945.

DEER SPIRIT   Miinike-giizis, the blueberry moon,
and an old warrior
travels through
the starry path of the Milky Way
up to the sacred abode
of the Great Spirit.
A child's vision
becomes the dream of life,
striving to do
what is honourable and right.

August 5, 1952
Francis Pegahmagabow is laid to rest.
Here is a story that does not end,
but continues today
in those who believe
in a country where justice will prevail,
as new generations rise up
to fill the footsteps of warriors
who have fallen long ago,
whose sacrifices and legacies
we continue to remember
and honour each November
across our vast home
and Native land.

A MOMENT OF SILENCE

AND

THEN

Sounding Thunder - Act III, Scene III - C Score

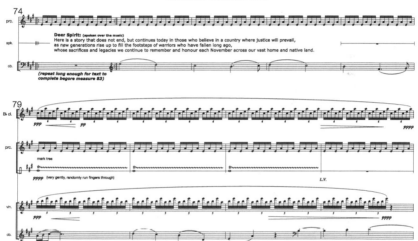

Deer Spirit: (spoken over the music)
Here is a story that does not end, but continues today in those who believe in a country where justice will prevail,
as new generations rise up to fill the footsteps of warriors who have fallen long ago,
whose sacrifices and legacies we continue to remember and honour each November across our vast home and native land.

131

Francis Reaches Out Slowly to Touch the Deer Spirit.

FRANCIS   In my dream I see a beautiful deer,
head raised,
nose up, ears twitching.
I approach from downwind,
but it turns to me,
and I realize
this is meant to be.
It is a spirit,
a Manido
in the body of a deer.

He Addresses the Spirit.

I know who you are.

WE ARRIVE AT THE BEGINNING AND ASK THE ENVITABLE QUESTION. ARE YOU READY? GIDOOZHIITAA NA?

A Kiss Among Kisses

About an hour and a half later, the performance at Wasauksing
First Nation is finished, and the audience is standing and clapping.
Some are calling out. Some have tears in their eyes.
Some are exchanging hugs. There are words of appreciation
and relief. The Chief stands to offer his remarks,
"Miigwech, Chi-Miigwech," he concludes.
Laura Pegahmagabow, a granddaughter of Francis, also stands
and offers a tearful thank you. Her voice trembles.
By now the artists are also teared up. Two years of hard work
from many hands have brought the project to completion.
The performance at Wasauksing is a triumph.
Sounding Thunder has taken off like a motorcycle courier
riding past the night watch.

Sounding Thunder: The Song of Francis Pegahmagabow's *closing moments
at the Wasauksing First Nation community centre. Photo courtesy of Mark Rush.*

[N]o problem is as consubstantial to literature and its modest mysteries as the one posed by translation.

– Jorge Luis Borges, "Las Versiones Homéricas," 1932

BALANCING ACT
GWYAKSEG EN'KAMGAK

A RETURN TO BEGINNINGS – HEREIN *SOUNDING THUNDER: THE SONG OF FRANCIS PEGAHMAGABOW*
GAA-BI-BDIKWEWDANG – BNAASWI PEGAHMAGABOW N'GAMWIN

Initial Performance
Wasauksing community centre, 20 July 2018
Wasauksing First Nation

Libretto by Armand Garnet Ruffo
Gaa-zhibii'ang Armand Garnet Ruffo

Music by Tim Corlis
Gaa-mnwewechgewin'ked Tim Corlis

Song contribution by Jennifer Kreisburg and Jodi Contin Baker
Gaa-wiidookaagejig negmowaad Jennifer Kreisburg and Jodi Contin Baker

Nishnaabemwin translation by Dr. Brian McInnes
Gaa-aan'kanootmaaged Brian McInnes

Cast and Roles
Ntam gaa-maandaagchigejig

Waawaate Fobister:
Francis Pegahmagabow, at various ages
Bnaaswi Pegahmagabow, bebkaan gaa-dso-bboon'gizid

Jennifer Kreisberg:
Deer Spirit
Waawaashkesh-Mnidoo

Larry Beckwith:
Multiple Voices: General/Officer; Lieutenant-Colonel Hill; Indian Agent; Reporter
Bebkaan Gaa-nitaagziig: Zhimaagnishiiw-gimaa; Gchi-zhimaag-nishiiw-gimaa; Indian Agent; Bebaamaajmod

Brian McInnes:
Narrator
Gaa-niigaanaan'gidood

Musicians
Ntam gaa-mdwewechgejig:

Jennifer Kreisberg:
Principal Singer
Gaa-niigaan'amaazod

Jodi Baker Contin:
Hand Drum, Supporting Vocals
Gaa-dewe'ged, Gaa-n'gamod

Larry Beckwith:
Conductor
Gaa-niigaanzid

James Campbell:
Clarinet
Bbigwan

Guy Few:
Trumpet
Boodaajgan

Mark Fewer:
Violin
Dooyaabiignignan

Beverley Johnston:
Percussion
Anooj mdwewechganan

James McKay:
Bassoon
Gchi-bbigwan

Joel Quarrington:
Double Bass
Gchi-naazhaabiig'igan

Rachel Thomas:
Trombone
Gchi-boodaajgan

Gabriel Cropley:
Stage and Lighting Designer, Projection Technician
Gaa-Nnaa'chiged

FAITH ACT
DEBWEWENDMING EN'KAMGAK

SCENE ONE
EKO-NTAMSING EZHWEBAK

(Francis is honouring the four directions. Music between each line.)
(Omnaajtoon niiwing wendaanmak maaba Bnaaswi. Mdwewemgad biitwi-yiing endso-zhibii'gaadegin.)

FRANCIS / BNAASWI

Wabenokkwe, keeper of the east.
Waabnookwe, Waabnong genwendang.

Shauwanigizik, keeper of the south.
Zhaawnoogiizhig, Zhaawnong genwendang.

Nanabush, keeper of the west.
Nenabosh, bngishmok genwendang.

Giyuedin, keeper of the north.
Giiwedin, Giiwednong genwendang.

SCENE TWO
EKO-NIIZHING EZHWEBAK

NARRATOR / GAA-NIIGAANAAN'GIDOOD

Spring 1915, the war has been raging on the Western Front for less than a year, and thanks to new technology – machine guns, tanks, airplanes, long-range artillery – tens of thousands of soldiers have already died in the slaughter.
Ziigwan 1915, gegaa go ngo-bboon gii-zhise iw gchi-miigaadwin bngishmok nakeyiing, njida go weshki-yaagin, nwi-baashkzignan, nwi-daabaanag, mbaas-jignag, waasa ezhaamgak nwi-baashkzignan, zaam niibwa zhimaagnishag gaa-nbojig.

Millions more will follow.
Washme gchi-baatiinwag wii-ni-nsindwaa.

Any thought of a quick end is now mired in mud and blood.
Kaa wewiib wii-shkwaasesinoon, mii dezhsing maa gpagjiishkweng miinwaa mskwiing.

To break the stalemate, the enemy turns to a new killing tool: chlorine gas.
Wii-ni-aanjsemgad, ogii-shki-aabjitoonaawaa gegoo neniizaanak mji-ninwag: gii-znagdoowaad bagdinaamwin.

And the Canadians are without masks.
Gaawiin bgidnaamochignan ogii-yaanziinaawaan giw Canadian zhimaag-nishag.

The first attack creates havoc, and General Edwin Alderson is desperate.
Gii-ggwaansagendaagwad eko-ntamising gaa-mwinewaawaad mii dash gii-zaamendang Gchi-zhimaagnishiiw-gimaa Edwin Alderson.

He approaches Francis Pegahmagabow.
Onaaskawaan Bnaaswi Pegahmagabowan.

GENERAL / GCHI-ZHIMAAGNISHIIW-GIMAA

The men have been talking about you.
Ggii-dzhimgoog giw ninwag.

FRANCIS / BNAAWSI

Sir.
Kiiwenz.

GENERAL / GCHI-ZHIMAAGNISHIIW-GIMAA

Is it true you can change the wind's direction?
Geget na gdaa-aanjtoon enaanmak?

FRANCIS / BNAAWSI

(Looking to the sky, pensive.)
(Giizhgong gii-naabi bebaamendang.)

I can try.
Ndaa-wiikjitoon.

GENERAL / GCHI-ZHIMAAGNISHIIW-GIMAA

(Hesitantly.)
(Beskaad.)

All right go ahead.
Ahaaw wi-doodan.

NARRATOR / GAA-NIIGAANAAN'GIDOOD

Change the wind?
Odaanjtoon na enaanmak?

The general wonders if what he asks, so curious and strange, is not indeed a sin.
Onaagdawendaan iw ggwedwed Gchi-zhimaagnishiiw-gimaa, ezhi-mya-gendaagwak, gii-maanaadak gye.

Without inhaling the tobacco, Francis makes his offering and asks the wind guardians to overtake the gas.
Gaawiin gii-wiiknaamsii semaans, gii-biindaakoojge maaba Bnaaswi wii-gwe-jmaad niw Mnidoon ge-zhaagoojtoonid.

FRANCIS / BNAAWSI

Spiritual order provides guidance:
Weweni ggii-kinoo'maagonaanig giw Mnidoog:

I put tobacco down on the earth to give prayers of humility and rebirth.
Nbagdinaa semaa maampii kiing ji-zhawenmiiyaang miinwaa ji-shki-bmaadzi-yaang.

NARRATOR / GAA-NIIGAANAAN'GIDOOD

Just before sunrise the wind changes from east to west, and the Germans suffer just as much as they do.
Gii-gwekaanmad jibwaa bi-mook'ang mii go naasaab gii-aanmizwaad giw megwenh-zhimaagnishag.

Like the Gete-nishnaabeg, the Indians of old, Francis's offering is accepted and heard by the spirit world.
Dbishkoo giw Gete-nishnaabeg, weweni ogii-daapnaawaan Mnidoog Bnaaswi odasemaan.

FRANCIS / BNAAWSI

"Chi-Miigwetch. Gitchi Manido."
"Chi-miigwech. Gchi-mnidoo."

SCENE THREE
EKO-NSING EZHWEBAK

NARRATOR / GAA-NIIGAANAAN'GIDOOD

Born in 1889, Francis Pegahmagabow, an Ojibwe boy, is now age two and like any other boy unaware what he will go on to do, but dark clouds appear on his horizon, upheaval the height of mountainous waves, grave enough to change the course of a child's life.
Gii-ndaadzi 1889, Bnaaswi Pegahmagabow, gii-Ojibwe-gwiiwzenswi, gaa-wiin mshi ogii-kendzii waa-ni-zhichged dbishkoo binoojiinwid gaa-niizho-bboon'gizid, aanwi go bi-mkadewaankwad wedi nakeyaa ge-ni-bmaadzid, gtaamgwaadkamig iw epiichi-mamaangaashkaamgak, ggwaansagaadkamik ge-aanji-bmaadzid maaba binoojiinh.

His father dies, his mother gravely ill, an adopted grandfather raises the boy, teaches him ceremony, custom and tradition.
Gii-nbowan odedeman, gii-gchi-aakziwan odoodooman, ogii-ntaawgi'goon omishoomsan gii-kinoo'maagod niw gete-nishnaabe-zhichgewinan.

Shaped by glory days of old, quest and vision, the sickly child takes it upon himself to entreat the help of the Sun Manido.
Gii-kinoo'maajgaazo gwyak gaa-maandaawchigewaad giw Gete-nishnaabeg, gaa-nji-ndawaabndang miinwaa gaa-nji-mkadeked, weweni gii-gaagiizmaad maaba binoojiinh gaa-aakzid niw Giisoo-Mnidoon.

He rises at dawn and runs from village to shoreline, training to be warrior strong.
Gii-gizhebaawii oodenaang biinish maa jiigbiig gii-bimbatood ji-mshkawziid naasaab gaa-mshkawziiwaad giw mnisnoog

Questions abound in breath and thought, afflict him like a cold winter night when the fire is low.
Gii-ggwedwe megwaa gii-nesed miinwaa gii-naagdawendang, dbishkoo gii-giikjid bboong megwaa dbasaakneg gaa-dbikdinig.

And so he asks, "What does it mean to be a great man, a brave man, a kind and honourable man, who will help save my people lest they parish, blown to the four directions?" Our beliefs a way of the past, our language gone deeper than the realm of Nzaagimaa, chief of the water serpents, vanished with the generations.
Ggwedwe dash, aaniish ge-zhi-aawid aw nini gchi-nendaagzid, zoongde'ed, miinwaa minwaadzid, wenesh waa-naadmawaad niw niijanishnaaben ji-maa-jaasinijin, niiwing wendaanmak gaa-webaashwaad, gegaa gii-webnigaadeg ezhi-debwewendmaang, washme giishkiindmaag gii-zhaamgad Nish-naabe-nwewin wedi endnakiid Nzaagimaa, mshi-gnebigo-gimaawi, gii-ngo-naagwad iw gaa-zhi-aan'ke-bmaadziwaad gow Nishnaabeg.

The boy now a young man sees that he must challenge and do battle, where battle is due.
Azhigwa maaba weshkinwewid miish gii-naagdawaabndang iw wii-nda-miigaadang.

Strength and deed becoming one, he becomes the voice of SOUNDING THUNDER.
Mshkawziiwin miinwaa zhichgewin gii-ni-bezhgong, gii-bi-bdikwewdang maa-ba gii-aawid.

SCENE FOUR
EKO-NIIWING EZHWEBAK

(The Deer Spirit appears. Francis holds up an imaginary rifle.)
(Gii-zhinaagzi aw Waawaashkesh-Mnidoo. Bzhishkonaamiinaage maaba Bnaaswi baashkzigan.)

FRANCIS / BNAAWSI

In my dream I see a beautiful deer, head raised, nose up, ears twitching.
Nbwaanaa waawaashkesh gwenaajwid, shpikweni, shpijaaneni, jjiibtawgeni.

I approach from downwind, but it turns to me, and I realize this is meant to be.
Ninaaskawaa maa niisaanmak, bi-gwekgaabwi ji-waabmid, mii dash iw gii-nji-kendmaan waa-zhiwebak.

It is a spirit, a Manido in the body of a deer.
Mnidoowi, aw Mnidoo ezhnaagzid waawaashkeshing.

(Addressing the deer.)
(Genoonaad waawaashkeshwan.)

I know who you are.
Gkenimin.

DEER SPIRIT / WAAWAASHKESH-MNIDOO

And so you do. I am your relative.
Gidebwe. Gdinwemin.

FRANCIS / BNAAWSI

Pegahmagabow, Caribou clan.
Begamigaabaw, Adik ndoodem

DEER SPIRIT / WAAWAASHKESH-MNIDOO

Gentle and swift, and yet strong and made to defend, these qualities in the body of a man.
Bekaadzi miinwaa gzhiikaabtoo, aanwi go mshkawzii ji-nitaa-gnawenjged, mii ezhi-miin'gozid aw nini wiiyaang.

Know that you have kin, human and other-than-human, to help you on your life path. Do it now, be done with the task.
Kendan eyaawadwaa gdinwendaagnag, Nishnaabewiwag miinwaa aanind Mnidoowiwag, ji-naadmookwaa ge-ni-bmoseyin, wi-doodan dash, giizhiikan iw.

FRANCIS / BNAAWSI

(He aims his rifle but cannot shoot.)
(Omzhodaan kaa dash gii-daa-baashkzigesii.)

I need to bring home food.
Ndaa-giiwewdoon miijim.

I know what it is like to nearly starve.
Gegaa ko ngii-gwanaandam.

DEER SPIRIT / WAAWAASHKESH-MNIDOO

I am Ogimâ, spirit chief of the deer,
Ndoogimaaw gow Waawaashkeshwag,

I give myself to you in this way.
Weweni gimiinin niiyaw.

Do what you must do.
Wi-doodan ge-ndawendman.

NARRATOR / GAA-NIIGAANAAN'GIDOOD

Travelling home with enough meat to feed hungry bellies the snow path breaks loose, and he loses his stride, tumbles down onto a frozen lake where he lies.
Ogiiwewdoon de-mnik wiiyaas ji-shamaad bekadenijin gii-biigse maanda miikaans maa gooning, mii dash iw gaa-nji-zhaashaakshing maa zaag'iganing gaa-gshkading.

A mighty crack issues and down he goes through the ice and into the frigid water.
Geskana go gii-daashkwading miish gii-dwaashing maa mkwamiiwaaboong.

DEER SPIRIT / WAAWAASHKESH-MNIDOO

Though you believe your death is near, and sing a brave song to allay your fear, it is not ours to predict when our time has come.
Mii sa iw enenman wiiba wii-ni-maajaayin, miinwaa ggwetaan'ganaandman ji-zegzisiwan, gaawiin gdaa-baamendziimin iwapii ge-ni-maajaaying.

I, guardian Manido, benevolent spirit, bid you to move back into the light of the sun.
Niin, nmnidoow, ngizhewaadiz gdaa-ggaanzomin wii-bi-zhe-giiweyin maa endzhi-minwaasged.

With a wave a turtle shall rise as though carrying the world; with a shake of his shell he throws you up and out as light as a snowflake falling about shore.
Mii ezhi-ndomind wii-bi-mooshkmo mshiikenh dbishkoo ggii-bmoomaan'-gonaan kina, gga-naangwebnig dbishkoo zoogpomgak maa jiigbiig ezhi-bapwi'ang odemkwaan.

Your feet now planted firmly on its back.
Gmashkawgaabaw maa biknaang.

FRANCIS / BNAAWSI

(Brushing himself off.)
(Jiishaagnedizo.)

I awake in the snow, and think my feet must have landed on rock, and I leaped with all my caribou strength.
Ngoshkos maa gooning, ndinendam gii-booniiyaan wedi siniing, mii dash gii-gwaashkoniyaan dbishkoo adikong.

Francis is now back in the village.
Gii-bi-zhe-giiwe oodenaang Bnaaswi.

FRANCIS / BNAAWSI

When they press me about spiritual matters, I shrug as though in half belief; I don't argue or fight.
Mii maanda pii bi-gwejmiwaad ezhi-mnidookeyaang, nbapwi-dinmaagne ndi-go ge debwewensiwaan, kaa gnage ndaagonwetasii.

I seek balance in a world both ancient and modern.
Aanwi go gwyakshkaayaan mewnzha miinwaa nongwa enkamigziying.

I press for support to go to school and learn to play the trumpet in a local brass band.
Aapji nnanddaan ji-ni-kinoo'maagziyaan miinwaa ji-mdwewetooyaan iw boo-daajgan biiwaabko-mdwewechgewining.

I'm twenty-one years old and free, living in a new century, and I sign on as a seaman to travel the Great Lakes.
Nniishtana-shi-bezhgo-bboon'giz, ezhi-bmaadziyaan weshki-dzhitaaying, ndaangbii'gaaz ji-naabkwaanshiin-ninwiyaan maa Gamiing.

SCENE FIVE
EKO-NAANING EZHWEBAK

(Francis waves a greeting and approaches a family of Ojibwe.)
(Gii-waawaatgoge miish gii-naaskawaad aanind Ojibwen.)

NARRATOR / GAA-NIIGAANAAN'GIDOOD

That summer they dock near Thunder Bay, and he joins a band of Ojibwe picking blueberries by the shore.
Gii-gwaabzowag besho Nimkii-wiikwedong gaa-niibing, mii dash gii-wiijiiwaad Ojibwen gii-baa-miin'kenijin maa jiigbiig.

He tells them his clan, and they are the same and they welcome him, share food and tell stories.
Owiindmawaan wedoodemid, mii dash gii-nkweshkwaawaad naasaab ezhi-doodemwaad, gii-wiidoopndiwag miinwaa gii-dbaajmotaadwag.

It is only when the Thunderbirds roar that they say goodbye and go their way, but not before an old Medicine Man among them speaks.
Mii eta go gii-maajaawaad pii gaa-noondaagzinijin niw Nimkiin, kawe gii-baa-biiwag ji-bi-gaagiigdod Mshkikiiwnini.

"Listen to the sounds above," he says.
"Weweni bzindan shpiming," kido.

"In one year's time such thundering you will hear, and in grave danger you shall be, but do not fear for I have something for you.
"Gga-noondaan iw baamaapii ngo-bboon, miinwaa gga-niizaanenmig, gego zegziken gegoo wii-miininaan.

"This medicine has come down from generations past and holds the power to protect you when you think all is lost."
"Waasa shkweyaang gii-njise maanda mshkiki ji-gnawenjgaazoyin gegaa gii-aanzhiitman."

(Francis touches the medicine sack around his neck.)
(Odaangnaan iw mshkikii-mshkmodens ezhi-biiskang Bnaaswi.)

NARRATOR / GAA-NIIGAANAAN'GIDOOD

He let the old Shaman be, and welcomed his medicine gift, for he did not want to offend and besides, he had learned years ago there is much to ponder and behold in the great mystery of the world.
Ogii-boon'aan Mshkikiiwniniwan, weweni gii-daapnang iw mshkiki ji-nshk'-aasig aanwi go, ogii-bi-kendaan niibwa eyaag ji-naanaagdawaabnjigaadeg kina ngoji maampii kiing.

FRANCIS / BNAAWSI

Chi-Miigwetch, thank you so much for your gift.
Chi-miigwech, gmiigwechwiyin maanda gii-miizhyin.

I am honoured and will wear it wherever I go.
Gbi-zhawenim miinwaa ge-biiskmaan kina ngoji ge-zhaayaan.

(He waves goodbye to the Shaman and arrives home on Parry Island.)
(Owaawaatge'aan mashkikiiwninwan mii dash gii-bi-zhe-giiwed maa Waa-saaksing.)

WAR ACT
GCHI-MIIGAADWIN EN'KAMGAK

SCENE ONE
EKO-NTAMSING EZHWEBAK

(Francis is now in front of a recruiting officer.)
(Bnaaswi nekweshkwaad niw nendwaangzhechgenid.)

NARRATOR / GAA-NIIGAANAAN'GIDOOD

Then he's back on his island home in time to witness the beginning of the darkest unknown, the greatest crime:
Mii dash gii-pi-giiwed maa mnising wenjbaad ji-bmi-waabndang gaa-maa-jii-bshagiishkaamgak kina gegoo, gchi-maanaaji-doodamwin gii-aawang:

when reason is abandoned to mankind's folly, and the great circle of life reflecting the promise of youth is shattered!
gii-ggiibaadaaknigewag iw gaa-webnamwaad naagdawendamwin, miinwaa gii-shigsing iw waa-zhi-mno-bmaadziwaad giw shki-nishnaabeg!

August 1914. Great Britain and Germany are at war, and within days Francis and thousands of other young men enlist.
Mnoomin'ke-giizis, 1914, gii-maajseni Great Britain miinwaa Germany omi-igaadwiniwaa, wiiba go gii-wiinzwin'kewag Francis miinwaa baatiinwag shkin-weg.

OFFICER / NIIGAANII-ZHIMAAGNISH

Let me get this straight, you insist on fighting a war that's not yours?
Nwii-nstotaan gwyak, gdaa-wii-dzhiikaan na iw megwenh-miigaadwin?

NARRATOR / GAA-NIIGAANAAN'GIDOOD

The officer looks him over begrudgingly and would rather send the Indian on his way.
Ogii-mji-gnawaabmaan niigaanii-zhimaagnish, wii-giiwenaashkawaad niw Nishnaaben ji-maajaanid.

But all the same Francis digs his heels in and explains why he and so many of his people feel compelled to do their part.
Odaagonwetaan aapji Bnaaswi, gii-wiindamaage iw wenji-zhichgewaad Nishnaabeg, waa-nji-dzhiikamwaad.

FRANCIS / BNAAWSI

It's my duty to serve king and country for there can be no denying the treaties my people made with Britain shall stand the test of time, now and forever, allies, nation to nation.
Ndaa-bimiitwaag Gchi-gimaa miinwaa gdakiimnaaning eyaajig gaawiin gdaa-aagonwetaziimin niw gchi-mzin'ignan gaa-zhitoowaad gow gaa-naaknigejig Nishnaabewakiing miinwaa Gete-zhaagnaashiiwakiing, nongwa miinwaa pane, wiijkiwendiying, gdakiiminaan miinwaa odakiimwaa.

NARRATOR / GAA-NIIGAANAAN'GIDOOD

A history that has gone unaware creates a pensive silence between the two men, harkens back to distant times, other wars and other enemies on Native land, when Indian allies swept down on rivers and changed the tide, the making of borders, the creation of a country.
Gaawiin weweni gii-kendaagwasinoon iw gaa-zhiwebak gaa-nji-bzaanziwaad giw niizh ninwag, dbishkoo mewnzha gaa-nakmigak, bebkaan miigaadwinan miinwaa bebakaan gaa-zhiingendaagzijig maampii Nishnaabewakiing, gii-bgamshkaawag Nishnaabeg maa ziibiing gegoo gaa-aanjtoowaad, gii-ki-mzin'igan'kewaad, weshki-zhichgaadeg Zhaagnaashiiwaki.

Pen in hand, Francis signs on, a pat on the shoulder, and he is like any other man.
Odaabjitoon zhibii'ganaak ji-daangbii'ang Bnaaswi, gii-baapaandin-maangne'ind, miinwaa gii-dbendaagzi gewiin.

To training camp off he goes, but what they don't know is he can shoot a hopping rabbit a good quarter-mile away.
Mii wedi endzhi-zhimaagnishiiwiwaad gaa-nji-zhaad, kaa gnage okendazii-naawaa ge-baashkzwaad waaboozoon gwaashkwanid ngoji go aabtawayiing aabta-diba'ganing.

OFFICER / NIIGAANII-ZHIMAAGNISH

(Sarcastically.)
(Ayaanwenmaad.)

So you want to be in the Northern Pioneers regiment?
Giwii-dibendaagos na Northern Pioneers regiment?

Odd for an Indian, but let's get on with it then: one, two, three! One, two, three, march!
Bkaan enaadzid aw Nishnaabe, maajtaadaa dash: bezhig, niizh, nswi! Bezhig, niizh, nswi, zhi-bmosen!

Now stand over there and let's see what you can do.
Wedi naaniibwin ji-waabndmaang maanda ge-gshktooyin.

Look down the road, see those target sheets, now load and shoot.
Naabin wedi miiknaang, waabndan niw mzhodami-mzin'ignan, wi-nash-knadoon, miinwaa baashkzigen.

NARRATOR / GAA-NIIGAANAAN'GIDOOD

It's during target practice that the officers take note.
Megwaa goji-baashkzigewin gii-naagdawaabmaawaad niigaanii-zhimaag-nishag.

They don't say anything but look on in surprise.
Gaawiin gegoo kidsiiwag meta go maamiikwaabndamwaad.

His great-grandfather, a warrior chief in 1812, must be the fighting instinct in the blood, they think.
Gii-mnisnoo-gimaawan niw odaan'kobjignan ngoji go 1812, mii dog iw mshkawziiwin eyaamgak mskwiing, enenmowaad.

Otherwise how to account for such an eye.
Aanwi dash gaa-nji-ntaa-waakwiid.

Moved to Valcartier training camp there's a surfeit of volunteers in these early recruiting days, and hundreds are sent home.
Mii maa Valcartier endzhi-ntaa-zhimaagnishiiwiwaad – aapji baatiinwag wii-daangbii'gewaad bijiinag gaa-maajseg,niibwa gii-giiwe-naazh'igaazwag.

A directive has come down forbidding Natives to fight, but that's all right, Lieutenant-Colonel F.W. Hill is tough as nails, and he looks for the hammer where he can find it.
Gii-bi-dgoshnoomgak maanda naaknigewin ge-nendaagzisigwaa Nishnaabeg ge-miigaazwaad, maanoo go iw, gii-aakwaadendaagzi aw Naagaanzid F.W. Hill, gii-gtaamgozi gegoo ezhichged miinwaa mekang.

LT.COL. F.W. Hill

Peggy, you're one of us!
Peggy, gdibenmigoo!

You'll stay and join the fight overseas.
Gga-baa-yaa wii-ni-wiijiiweying wedi gaamiing.

FRANCIS / BNAAWSI

They call me one of them, but I remember the old Medicine Man near Thunder Bay.
Zhimaagnish ndigoo, nmikwenmaa dash aw Mshkikiiwnini besho Nimkii-wii-kwedong.

I welcomed his medicine gift because I sensed it contained a kind of power few today acknowledge, or truly understand.
Ngii-mnodaapnaan iw gii-moozhtooyaan gaa-nji-mnidoowaadak, bangiishen-gizwag geyaabi kendmoog maage nsidotmoog.

SCENE TWO
EKO-NIIZHING EZHWEBAK

DEER SPIRIT / WAAWAASHKESH-MNIDOO

In the trenches, in the muck, in the stench of death, the young soldiers come to believe in something greater than what they see, greater than themselves, greater than cannon and shell in all that they witness in their hell.
Mii   gaa-dzhi-waan'kewaad,   gaa-gpagjiishkweng   gaa-nichiiwmaagok,

gii-bi-debwewendmoog giw shki-zhimaagnishag gegoo washme gaa-waab-ndamwaad, washme gaa-aawiwaad, washme gaa-baashkzigaadeg ngoji endapnewaad.

Ordered to continue to the last man, they want nothing more than to understand.
Gii-noonindwaa iw ji-jaagnewaad, meta go wii-nisdotamwaad.

Down on their knees, or standing tall, they look to the sky, the universe, so large and they so small.
Gii-jiingnitaawag gemaa gii-naaniibwiwag, gii-naabwag giizhgong, gaagge-giizhig, chi-mchaagmad, gii-gchi-gaashiinyag.

Francis is in the trenches.
Gii-yaa maaba Bnaaswi gaa-dzhi-waan'kewaad.

NARRATOR / GAA-NIIGAANAAN'GIDOOD

The 1st Battalion arrives in Europe and marches steadfast into Belgium, arrives at a spot of ground called Ypres, still not claimed by the Germans.
Shki-dgoshnoog maa Gaaming eko-ntamsing Battalion gii-zhi-bmosewag gwyak maa Belgium-ing, ngoji gii-dgoshnoog Ypres, ezhnikaadeg kaa mshi gii-dakiimsiiwag Germany wenjibaajig.

But to their horror the Canadians find they are totally unprepared for the war; none have experienced anything like this ever before:
Gii-gwaansagendmoog giw Canada zhimaagnishag gaa-zhiitaasigook maa miigaading, gaawiin wiikaa gegoo ogii-zhi-kendaziinaawaa:

a foot of sewer water in the trenches, surrounded by razor-sharp barbed wire fences, a steady barrage of artillery fire dropping upon the men, the shells disinter the bodies, then bury them again.
ngo-zid moowaaboo eyaamgak gaa-dzhi-waan'kewaad, gii-giiwtaawaa-biigad niw giinaa-mchikanan, gii-miikshkoozowag ninwag gaa-aabji-mdwewezgemgak, gii-mookamgiseniwan niw wiiyawaan miish miinwaa gii-niishkamgisenigin.

Sniper bullets zinging overhead, while ghostly flares illumine the dead, over six thousand cylinders of gas released in the air; soldiers vomiting, turning green, running scared; a stalemate of armies dug in like dung beetles fatly fed on a daily ration of blood meal.
Gii-mdwewewan niwiin wedi shpiming, megwaa gii-zhinaagziwag giw

gaa-nbojig waasgonechgaansing, obagdinaawaan 6,000 moodyan maa shpiming; gii-shagwewag, gii-aakziiwnaagziwag, gii-maajiibtoowag; bebkaanziwaad zhimaagnishag gaa-yaajig dbishkoo giw mnidooshag gaa-ntaa-miijwaad mskwi.

OFFICER / NIIGAANII-ZHIMAAGNISH

Stand-to, wait for the whistle.
Zhigaabwig, baabiitoog iw gwiishkojgan.

Bayonets fixed, we're going over the top, shoulder to shoulder!
Gii-zhinoo'gemgadoon baashkzignan, gibaashjigaakiiwebtoomin, ezhi-wiijbatooying!

FRANCIS / BNAAWSI

We run straight into a storm of machine gun bullets, no turning back, so we bend into it like it's hail.
Nbimbatoomin maa gwyak gaa-baapaashkzodiwaad, gaawiin ndaa-bskaabbatoosiimin, nbitaakshkaamin dbishkoo mkwamiibiisaag.

Then the mortar begins, shrapnel razing the ground.
Mii dash gii-maajii-baapaashkideg, gii-bnaadak kina gegoo maa kiing.

Every second man in the 1st and 4th Divisions goes down.
Aabta giw gaa-yaajig gii-nsindwaa maa eko-ntamsing miinwaa eko-niiwing Divisioning.

How can you trust an officer after that?
Aaniish nongwa ge-debwewenmad aw niigaanii-zhimaagnish gaa-nakmigak?

OFFICER / NIIGAANII-ZHIMAAGNISH

That's all right, boys, we'll get them next time.
Weweni nenmoog shkinwedog, baamaapii gga-debnaanaanig.

FRANCIS / BNAAWSI

Thompson, Hall and Chapelle too, I watch them die and learn quick enough, there's little I can do.
Thompson, Hall miinwaa Chapelle, nwaabmaag gaa-zhi-nbowaad ji-kenmaan, kaa aapji gegoo ndaa-zhichgesii.

Boys, spilling out their guts, who call for their mothers.
Shkinweg, gii-mzhwindwaa gii-aano-gnoonaawaad niw odoodoomwaan.

OFFICER / NIIGAANII-ZHIMAAGNISH

The only way to win this war is to fight fire with fire.
Meta go daa-wii-ntaawaakwiiying ji-gshktooying maa gchi-miigaading.

I call for snipers to go out at night and gather information on the enemy.
Nnandmaag giw gaa-giimooji-baashkzigejig ji-niibaashkaawaad ge-gii-
moozaabmaawaad.

Claim the Hun by speed or stealth, bullet or knife, the work needs to be done.
Debish aw mji-ninwishag ge-gzhiikaabtooyin gemaa ge-giimooj'adwaa, nwi
maage mookmaan, daa-giizhichgaadeg maanda nokiiwin.

FRANCIS / BNAAWSI

He calls it work, but I've known work since I was a child.
Owiindaan nokiiwin, ndanokii gaa-ko-binoojiinwiyaan.

I know hunting too.
Nnitaa-giiyose gaye.

This he orders is something else.
Mii go bkaan ezhi-noonaad.

OFFICER / NIIGAANII-ZHIMAAGNISH

Peggy, it's up to you.
Peggy, gidaa-zhichge.

FRANCIS / BNAAWSI

Yes, Sir!
Geget, Kiiwenz!

NARRATOR / GAA-NIIGAANAAN'GIDOOD

Then it's April, springtime, a time of flowers and new growth, but it's 1916, and
the number of dead float in the air like tiny droplets of dew.

Skigmizge-Giizis, Ziigwan, pii baashkaabgoniig miinwaa eshkging, azhigwa 1916, mii endshiwaad giw gaa-nbojig ndigo ge endsingin gaa-wanbiisaamgak.

How do you make sense of it?
Aaniish ge-nisdotaman?

133,000 French; 100,000 British, including Canadians; 120,000 Germans; and on and on, until the little drops of dew become an ocean, and mean little or nothing, unless it's someone you knew.
133,000 Wemtigoozhiig; 100,000 Zhaagnaashag, degon'gaazwaad Canada wenjbaajig; 120,000 Germany wenjbaajig; geyaabi aanind miinwaa aanind, naangim maa gamii gaa-ayaamgak, gaawiin gegoo nendaagwasinoon, ge maage wiya gaa-zhi-kenmad.

OFFICER / NIIGAANII-ZHIMAAGNISH

A fine job done.
Ggii-wiingez.

I'm putting you up for a commendation.
Gga-wiidookoon ge-nsidwaabmik.

But why are you such a loner?
Aaniish wenji-nshikewziyin?

FRANCIS / BNAAWSI

I go out with others at first.
Kawe nwiijiiwaag aanind.

I turn to my partner but he only has half a head, and I come back alone and swear: no spotter for me from that point on.
Ndinaab'aa nwiijiiwaagan meta go aabta-shtigwaned, nbi-zhe-bezhig miish gii-zhi-baataajmoyaan: kaa geyaabi wiya dekwaabndang wii-naadmawid.

OFFICER / NIIGAANII-ZHIMAAGNISH

I see a few of the men behaving like you and putting down tobacco.
Nwaabmaag aanind ezhichgewaad naasaab ezhichgeyin gaa-bagdineg semaa.

This is a Christian war, by George!
Maanda Gchi-nam'e-miigaadwin, shke Jaaj!

What are these things you do?
Wegnesh now ezhichgeyin?

FRANCIS / BNAAWSI

Look around, the constant bombing has turned the land into a graveyard, skeleton trees marking the dead.
Baa-naabin, gchi-n'gokaan yaawang maampii kiing gaa-nji-baashknejiisjige-waad, gow mtigooshag gii-zhinoowaawaan niw gaa-nbonijin.

I take a piece of one of the branches, put it in my month and become the grey earth.
Nbi-gonendaan iw dikwaans ji-zhinaagziyaan dbishkoo gaa-waabkamgaak.

My medicine is strong, and I feel invisible, invincible.
Geget zoongan nmshkikiim, ndoonji-n'gwaabminaagos, ndoonji-maandaawiz.

OFFICER / NIIGAANII-ZHIMAAGNISH

You're a good soldier, Pegahmagabow, but you're a rather big swell!
Gnitaa-zhimaagnishiiw, Pegahmagabow, ggotaamgos!

FRANCIS / BNAAWSI

The Military Medal, and I am treated like a new recruit.
Gchi-biiwaabkoons, ndoodaagoog dbishkoo gii-shki-zhimaagnishiiwiyaan.

OFFICER / NIIGAANII-ZHIMAAGNISH

As your new commanding officer, I simply can't believe your report.
Mii weshki-gimaawiyaan, gaawiin ndebweyendaziin gaa-bi-wiindmaageyin.

FRANCIS / BNAAWSI

When you get killed or captured, you'll believe it.
Pii dash nesigooyin gemaa debnigooyin, gga-debweyendaan.

OFFICER / NIIGAANII-ZHIMAAGNISH

I could have you arrested for that.
Gdaa-gii-dkon'goo iw ekdoyin.

FRANCIS / BNAAWSI

I was in the trenches before you even signed on.
Ngii-yaanaaban gaa-dzhi-waan'kewaad jibwaa gii-biijbii'geyin.

OFFICER / NIIGAANII-ZHIMAAGNISH

You're out of line.
Ggiibaadiz.

FRANCIS / BNAAWSI

Maybe yes, maybe no.
Gnabach geget, gnabach gaawiin.

But what I do know is my job is to scout and snipe and take the enemy out, and
I'm the best at what I do.
Ndoonji-kendaan, nnitaawchige ge-ndawaatooyaan miinwaa ge-giimooji-
baashkzwagwaa giw mji-ninwag.

With my Ross rifle and scope I count over three hundred targets.
Ndaabjitoon maanda Ross-baashkzigan miinwaa debaabnjigan ji-gimagwaa
washme 300 gaa-yaajig.

I see in the crosshairs flesh and blood, just like me and you!
Nwaabndaanan maa debaabnjigning ozhag'ay miinwaa mskwi, dbishkoo gii-
nwind!

NARRATOR / GAA-NIIGAANAAN'GIDOOD

The war takes its toll like a disease from which nobody is immune, leaving
both soldiers and countries in ruins.
Mii go dbishkoo naapnewin gii-aawan iw miigaadwin – kina wiya zhi-naa-
pnewaad gaa-bnaadak kina gegoo – zhimaagnishag miinwaa Akiin.

Another year, hundred-pound shells, 65,000 tonnes fired at Passchendaele.
Ngo-bboon geyaabi, 100 dbaabiishkoojganan gchi-nwiin, 65,000 gchi-dbaa-biishkoojganan ogii-baashkzaanaawaa maa Passchendaeling.

Stalemate on both sides, everybody fails.
Gii-aano-wiikjitoowaad, gii-aanwewziwaad kina wiya.

November 1917, the Canadians finally take it.
Gshkadino-giizis 1917, ogii-debnaanaawaa maanda Canada wenjbaajig.

Total losses on the British side: some 245,000 men, not counting the French and the Germans.
Mii mnik gaa-ni'aawaad Zhaagnaashag: 245,000 ninwan, geyaabi go aanind Wemtigoozhiig miinwaa Germany wenjbaajig.

And then Peggy gets shot in the leg and sent to England to recuperate.
Mii dash gii-baashkzwind maa kaading Peggy gii-maajiinaazhkawaad wedi Gete-Zhaagnaashiiwakiing ji-noojmod.

SCENE THREE
EKO-NSING EZHWEBAK

FRANCIS / BNAAWSI

When they ask me about getting wounded I tell them I lost my faith.
Niwiindmawaag gaa-debwewendsiwaan pii gwejmiwaad gaa-nji-miikshkoozyaan.

It's difficult to keep it in a place like this.
Znagad wii-bmwidooyin maampii nake.

With it went the tiny medicine bag given to me by the old Shaman.
Ngii-nitoon gye iw mshkikii-mshkimodens gaa-miizhid aw mshkikiiwnini.

Sometimes it felt hard as rock, at other times like it contained nothing!
Naan'godnong gii-mshkawaa, aapiichin go gii-bzhishgon!

NARRATOR / GAA-NIIGAANAAN'GIDOOD

As soon as he's physically able he's back on the front and in the thick of it.
Mii maa niigaaning wewiip ezhaad gaa-nji-gshktood.

But he's not the same, not as stable they say, and he's sent to Lord Derby War
Hospital where they look for what's wrong but they know all along.
Gaawiin naasaab aawisii, gaawiin aapji mno-yaasii, kidwag,gii-maajii-
naazha'wind wedi Lord Derby Gchi-aakzi-gamgoong ji-gnawaabmind, mii ko
gii-kendmowaad gaa-nji-zhiwebzid.

The average life in the trenches is six months.
Mii eta go aabta-bboon ge-ni-dzhi-bmaadzid wedi niigaaning.

He's been dug in for nearly four years!
Gii-dzhitaa ngoji go niiyo-bboon!

HOMEFRONT ACT
ENDAANG EN'KAMGAK

SCENE ONE
EKO-NTAMSING EZHWEBAK

DEER SPIRIT / WAAWAASHKESH-MNIDOO

What about those who no one sees, those with no shattered bones or missing limbs, a wound whose roots go deeper than the tallest, majestic tree.
Wenesh giw gaa-gwiinwaabminaagzijig, gaawiin gii-bookokanesiiwag maage gaa-nitoosigook okaadan, onikan ge, gii-wiisgendaagwad washme gii-gnwaa-biigdoon niw jiibkan gchi-mtigong.

Let us mourn for the ones who died, were resurrected and returned, abandoned and forgotten, in a country they no longer recognized.
Gga-gshkendaamin enenmangwaa giw gaa-maajaawaad, gaa-aabjiibaawaad, gaa-zhe-giiwewaad, gaa-webnigaazwaad miinwaa gaa-wnenjigaazwaad, maa Kiing nesidwinaajgesigook.

(Francis is standing at attention with a Military Medal pinned to his chest.)
(Zhigaabwi maaba Francis gii-zgaakw'ind Gchi-biiwaabikoons kaaknaang.)

NARRATOR / GAA-NIIGAANAAN'GIDOOD

April 1919, and Francis Pegahmagabow returns a hero.
Nmebni-giizis 1919, gii-bi-wedaasewid Bnaaswi Pegahmagabow.

He has sniped 378 of the enemy and has virtually lasted the duration of the war.
Ogii-giimooji-baashkzwaan 378 megwen-zhimaagnishan, gegaa go gii-zhaab-shkang gbey'iing gchi-miigaading.

The Military Medal and two bars directly from the Prince of Wales; he is far from a regular soldier sliding unnoticed into the ranks of civilian life.
Ogii-miin'goon nso-biiwaabkoonsan niw Gchi-gimaansan, washme go ezhi-zhimaagnishiiwid maaba gaa-bi-zhe-giiwed.

He moves back to the island of Wasauksing determined to pick up where he left off.

Gii-bi-aanjgozi neyaap Waasaaksing ezhi-getnaamendang ji-zhe-mno-bmaadzid.

He soon marries and children are born.
Wiiba go ogii-wiidgemaan miish gii-yaawaawaad oniijaansiwaan.

Life has never been better, and yet for him there is still the storm rising on great wings.
Aapji dash gii-mno-bmaadzid, aanwi go gii-bi-gtaamgod gezkemgak.

FRANCIS / BNAAWSI

I brush off my uniform and take up arms and patrol the reserve roads at night.
Ngii-zhe-mmoonan nzhimaagnishii-gwiwnan miinwaa baashkzigan ji-bim-saadamaan niw miiknan shkonganing megwaa dbikak.

I'm determined to protect my wife and children.
Nga-kawaabmaag ndikwem miinwaa nniijaansag.

The neighbours open their curtains and wonder what I'm doing.
Giimooji-dapaabwag waasechganing niijanishnaabemag ji-naagdawaabmi-waad.

How do I explain what I still see – magnified just for me!
Aaniish naa ge-waawiindmaageyaan geyaabi waabndamaan – niin eta gii-nsidwinaajgeyaan!

REPORTER / BEBAAMAAJMOD

Mr. Pegahmagabow,
Begamigaabaw,

Is it true what they're saying?
Geget na ekdowaad?

Over three hundred sniped! How is it possible?
Washme 300 gaa-nsindwaa! Aaniish ge-zhiwebdogwen?

FRANCIS / BNAAWSI

I had help.
Ngii-wiidookaagoo.

REPORTER / BEBAAMAAJMOD

What do you mean?
Aaniish iw ekdoyin?

FRANCIS / BNAAWSI

There's always help if we believe: one night we were overtaken, not by guns, but by a terrific thunderstorm.
Gwiidookaagonaan pane debweyendming: ngii-dimne'goomin ngo-dbikad gaa-nimkiikaamgak, gaawiin baashkzignan.

I felt the air flap around my face, and I was shaken by the wings of a mighty bird.
Ngii-moozhtoon gaa-wewebaasing maa ndengwaang, miish gaa-nangwebnid aw bemsed gchi-bnesi.

I knew at that instant I was in the midst of what we call Biidweyaangwe, the coming sound of a Thunderbird's wings!
Ngii-kendam iwapii gaa-biidweyaangwed, gaa-bi-noondaagzinijin bnesi on-ingwii'gnan!

REPORTER / BEBAAMAAJMOD

Well, you don't say.
Geget na gdikid.

SCENE TWO
EKO-NIIZHING EZHWEBAK

(Francis is meeting an agent of the Indian Department.)
(Bnaaswi nayaaskawaad enokiinid Indian Departmenting.)

NARRATOR / GAA-NIIGAANAAN'GIDOOD

The first thing Francis realizes is the gulf between cultures is as wide as the Great Lakes.
Mii go ntam nesdotang Bnaaswi ezhi-bkaanak niw zhitwaawinan mnik ekwaakin niw Gamiin.

Some are quick to comment that his record must be fake, but even more pressing is the lack of respect. A primitive people, they say, who cannot manage their own affairs.
Gii-bi-dzhindmoog iw gaa-nibii'gaazod, kaa gnage ogii-piitenmaasiwaawaan, Nishnaabewishag, ekdowaad, ge-gnawendzosigook.

FRANCIS / BNAAWSI

I'd like a loan to buy a cow from old Mrs. Keeshig.
Nwii-wi'igoo zhoon'yaa ji-yaajgeyaan mndmooyenh Keeshig obizhkiiman

AGENT

A waste of money.
Gwebnaa zhoon'yaa.

FRANCIS / BNAAWSI

I can sell the extra milk.
Ndaa-daawen iw doodooshaaboo.

AGENT

Someone will knock on your door in need. And there it goes.
Wii-bi-detewaakwige wiya maa gdishkwaandeming. Mii dash wii-maa-jaamgak.

FRANCIS / BNAAWSI

A cow will give my family a head start.
Nga-wiidookaagonaan ndanwendaagnag aw bzhiki.

AGENT

I can get you a job fixing roads, cutting railway ties.
Gdaa-noonin ji-miiknaakeyin, ge-jiigga'geyin.

FRANCIS / BNAAWSI

My lungs suffer from the war.
Nbiipiisdeg gaa-aakziishkaagong njida iw gchi-miigaading.

AGENT

Well then, I'll see what I can do. Time's up, I'll get back to you.
Ahaaw dash, nga-naagdawaabndaan. Mii iw mnik, gga-zhe-gnoonin.

NARRATOR / GAA-NIIGAANAAN'GIDOOD

A loan to buy a cow, a team of horses, a farm under the Soldier Settlement Act,
the Indian Agent scoffs and scorns and won't support Francis's application.
Zhoon'yaa wii-wi'ind ji-yaawaad bzhkiwan, niw bezhgoogazhiin, gtigaan wen-
dnang Soldier Settlement Act, gii-goopdendang Indian Agent maa nwewe-
tood, gaawiin wii-naadmawaasiin Bnaaswiwan.

He tells the government Francis is too much of a risk, too temperamental, not
right in the head; just because the man's a veteran, doesn't mean he should
expect compensation.
Ogii-wiindmawaan niw gchi-gimaan ezhi-goopdizid, zaam nshkaadzi,
aabtawaadzi; gii-aano-zhimaagnishiwiiban, gaawiin memkaach daa-miingosii
zhoon'yaa.

Turned away again and again, even with the Band's support, Francis wonders
what his sacrifice was all about.
Gii-anwenmind niibwa daching, gii-aano-wiidookaagod owiijanishnaabeman,
gii-naanaagdawendang Bnaaswi gaa-gchi-miigwed.

FRANCIS / BNAAWSI

Equality in the trenches in a time of need, but now I'm back to the end of the
line with barely enough to feed my family.

Mii ko naasaab enenmigooyaang wenji-miigaading gaa-yaayaang, gaawaanh go nongwa ge-ni-shamadwaa ndanwendaagnag ndigo ge eshkwegaabwiyaan.

NARRATOR / GAA-NIIGAANAAN'GIDOOD

A time when everything Indian is banned and shunned, his people are subject to the whim of the Indian Department, which hands out Band payments like a child's allowance.
Mii iwapii gaa-aanwendaagwak kina gegoo Nishnaabe-bmaadziwining, dbish-koo binoojiinwiwaad gii-doodwindwaa Nishnaabeg ezhi-dba'amaagowaad.

At one time owning the whole Parry Sound region and more, Waaseyaakos-ing, "the place that shines brightly in the reflection of sacred light," and then deceived.
Ngoding gii-dakiimwag kina ngoji maa Parry Sounding, Waaseyaakosing, "ngoji gii-waaseyaamgak gaa-dzhi-mnidoowaasgegwen" mii dash gii-wyezh-mindwaa.

Even their tiny island home is taken without compensation.
Ogii-bi-mkamaagowaan Nishnaabeg ngoji gaa-daawaad.

J.R. Booth, king of the Ottawa Valley lumber barons with influential govern-ment connections, gets hundreds of acres for his Atlantic Railway depot.
J.R. Booth, gii-niigaanziikdawaan niw gaa-giishk'aakwenjin Ottawa Valleying, gii-miinind niibwa daswaakakiins ji-shkode-daabaan-miiknaaked.

His last request: burn his papers, cover his tracks.
Mii iw shkwaach gii-nanddang: jaagzan omzin'iganan, gaadoon gaa-zhichged.

Francis realizes straight away something must be done!
Ogii-kendaan gwyak gegoo da-zhiwebak!

(Francis is addressing the Indian Agent.)
(Bnaaswi genoonaad Indian Agentan.)

FRANCIS / BNAAWSI

The Canadian National Lumber and Tie Company is cutting all the valuable timber on the reserve and not giving us anything.
Giishk'aakwewag kina gegoo shkon'ganing giw Canadian National Lumber and Tie Company enokiijig – kaa gegoo nmiin'goosiimin.

We want it stopped.
Nndawendaamin iw ji-boontoowaad.

AGENT

The Indian Department would have to approve it.
Odaa-gii-daapnaanaawaa iw Indian Department enokiijig.

FRANCIS / BNAAWSI

That's why I'm here.
Mii wenji-yaayaan.

AGENT

Duly noted.
Gii-naanaagdawenjigaadeg.

FRANCIS / BNAAWSI

And our beautiful Sandy Island?
Gmnisnaan gwenaajwang Sandy Island?

And Shkodeng-mnis, the place where the spirits live?
Shkodeng-mnis, endnakiiwaad Mnidoog?

It was never in the treaty.
Gaawiin gii-zhibiigaadesinoon treaty-mzin'iganing.

White people are building summer homes there.
Odoozhitoonaawaan niw niibno-wiigwaaman wedi Zhaagnaashag.

AGENT

Well, I'll see what I can do. Time's up, I'll get back to you.
Nga-naagdawendaan iw. Mii iw nongwa. Gga-zhe-gnoonin.

127

DEER SPIRIT / WAAWAASHKESH-MNIDOO

Francis prays to the Great Spirit.
Bnaaswi gyaagiizmaad Gchi-Mnidoon.

Beseeches the Manidos for intervention.
Onandmaan niw Mnidoon ji-wiidookaagowaad.

Attends the Catholic mass devoutly.
Nitaa-nam'aa wedi Gchi-nam'ewgamigong.

Prays to Jesus Christ who sent a nun to care for him when he thought he would lose his leg.
Begsenmaad Zhezasan gii-maajiinizhaagod nam'e-kwe ji-gnawenmigod gegaa gaa-nitood okaad.

NARRATOR / NIIGAANAAN'GIDOOD

And still the iron fist of the Indian Department beats down.
Geyaabi go ozaam-gimaakndawaan niw Nishnaaben.

Francis is desperate for change and runs for Chief, but the government calls the shots, and there's not a lot the Band can do, except write letters and pass Council resolutions, and then Francis comes up with a solution.
Gii-ggetnaamendam wii-gimaawid Bnaaswi gegoo ji-aanjseg, geyaabi go de-baaknigewaad giw Zhaagnaashag, gaawiin aapji gegoo daa-gshkitoosiinaawaa Nishnaabeg, meta go wii-zhibii'amwaad mzin'iganan miinwaa wii-naaknige-waad, mii dash gii-bi-kendang Bnaaswi ge-ni-gwyaksidood.

He starts organizing politically and joins the newly formed Brotherhood of Canadian Indians, and helps establish the National Indian Government.
Ogii-dzhiikaan iw dbaakniwewin miinwaa gii-bi-dbendaagzid maanda shki-ya'ii Brotherhood of Canadian Indians, miinwaa gii-wiidookaaged ge-zhich-gaadeg maanda National Indian Government.

(Francis addressing the Indian Agent.)
(Bnaaswi genoonaad Indian Agentan.)

FRANCIS / BNAAWSI

We want our rights.
Nwii-yaamin gaa-miin'goziying.

128

AGENT

Order under the British flag above all.
Gmno-zhiwebzimin naamyi'ii Gchi-gimaa-kewwining.

FRANCIS / BNAAWSI

Then we'll bypass Indian Affairs and go directly to King George
Nga-dimne'aamin Indian Affairs ge-ni-naaskwangid Gchi-gimaa Jaaj.

AGENT

I'll remove you as Chief.
Gga-bagdinin wegimaawiyin.

FRANCIS / BNAAWSI

For what reason?
Aaniish wenji-zhichgeyin?

AGENT

Incompetence. You're of no value to me, or the Band.
Ggoopdis. Gaawiin gnage gdapiitendaagoosii niin maage giijanishnaabemag.

FRANCIS / BNAAWSI

I'll hire a lawyer.
Nga-noodmawaa aw gnoodmaagenini

AGENT

Lawyers cost money.
Shpangzowag giw genoodmaagejig.

FRANCIS / BNAAWSI

I'll raise the money.
Nga-zhoon'yaake.

AGENT

It's against the law.
Gaawiin nendaagwasinoon naaknigewining.

FRANCIS / BNAAWSI

I'll fight.
Nga-miigaadaan.

AGENT

Listen, the majority want things to stay the way they are.
Nshke, gegaa kina wiya ezhi-ndawendamwaad iw noongwa eyaamgak.

FRANCIS / BNAAWSI

Because the government holds back Band payments if we don't stay quiet.
Njida go diba'maagosiwangid giishpin bzaanzisiwaang.

AGENT

Time's up. Got to go.
Mii iw nongwa. Ndaa-maajaa.

SCENE THREE
EKO-NSING EZHWEBAK

NARRATOR / GAA-NIIGAANAAN'GIDOOD

Then it is over.
Mii sa iw eshkwaakmigak

Francis is voted out of office.
Gii-zaagjiwebnind Bnaaswi gaa-nji-gimaawid.

He joins the peacetime militia and feels the old camaraderie again, his medals pinned to his chest. Equality and fraternity in the khaki uniform, he is greeted as one of the best.
Ogii-bi-dzhiikaan iw bzaan-teg zhimaagnishag ezhichgewaad miinwaa ogii-kendaan iw zhi-ngadendiwin, ogii-zgaakwa'aanan niw biiwaabkoon ezhi-kendang mno-doodaadwin miinwaa wiijkiiwendiwin zhimaagnishii-gwi-wining, gii-nimkawind aapji gaa-wiingezid.

For a while he's an ambassador for the military.
Jina go gii-mzhinwewi iw gaa-dbendaagziwaad zhimaagnishag.

In procession he stops to comfort a mother who has lost two sons in the war.
Gii-nooggaabwi maaba gaa-maajiiyaawnidwag ji-gaagiij'aad niw kwewan gaa-ni'god ogwisan gchi-miigaading.

DEER SPIRIT / WAAWAASHKESH-MNIDOO

Though we think we know what really matters, we live in the world of souls and shadows;
Gdinendaamin iw enendaagwak, gbmaadzimin ngoji yaawag mnidoog miin-waa jiibyag;

Intervention comes when we least expect it.
Gnaadamaagoomin ge-dnendanziwing.

Around us human and spirit, the known and the unknown, a snap of a finger, and we are in their midst.
Bbaa-yaawag bemaadzijig miinwaa Mnidoog, iw kendaagwad miinwaa iw kendaagwasinoon, chi-geskana, ge-wiijiiwangwaa.

NARRATOR / GAA-NIIGAANAAN'GIDOOD

His militia work too comes to an end.
Gii-boontoon iw gaa-zhimaagnishiiwid.

And with support from the military Francis is finally given a disability pension.
Gii-miinind iw maakzi-zhoon'yaa Bnaaswi gaa-nenmigod owiiji-zhimaag-nishan.

But still under the yoke of Indian Affairs, no veteran benefits for him.
Mii dash iw enenmowaad Indian Affairs, enokiijig kaa gnage veteran benefits
gii-wiidookaagosiin Bnaaswi.

Always one step behind, or one step ahead, the Indian department still calls
the shots, continues to put up roadblocks to curtail treaty rights, human rights.
Pane ngo-dkokiiwin shkweyaang, gemaa ngo-dkokiiwin niigaaning geyaabi go
debaaknigewaad Indian department enokiijig, gebshkawaawaad Nishnaaben
wii-yaamwaad Nishnaabe-miin'go'ewziwin.

For Francis, it has always been the good fight.
Pane go naa gaa-ntaa-miigaadang Bnaaswi.

Francis is worn out and pensive.
Gii-shkwaabza miinwaa gii-mgitoo Bnaaswi.

FRANCIS / BNAAWSI

I like to spend my time with my family now.
Nmnwendaan netaa-wiijiiwagwaa ndanwendaagnag nongwa.

I take my children to church, and we sing the old hymns.
Ndizhwinaag nniijaansag maa Nam'ewgamgong ji-nam'e-n'gamoyaang.

I also teach them what's important – our language and our ceremonies, the
land, the things we need to take care of.
Nkinoo'mawaag kina epiitendaagwok enweyaang, mnidookeyaang, miinwaa
ki, kina gegoo ge-gnawendmaang.

People still come asking for help.
Bi-ggwedwewag aanind wii-wiidookwindwaa

I do what I can.
Ndoodaan mnik geshktooyaan.

And then there are those who offer help.
Wii-bi-naadmaagewag aanind.

It is good to have faith.
Nishin aapji de-debwewendming.

DEER SPIRIT / WAAWAASHKESH-MNIDOO

Miin'ke-giizis, the blueberry moon, and an old warrior travels through the starry path of the Milky Way up to the sacred abode of the Great Spirit.
Miin'ke-giizis, pii miin'kewaad giizsoong, gii-zhaa maaba gete-mnisnoo maa Nenabosho-miiknaang biinish maa endnakiid Gchi-Mnidoo.

A child's vision becomes the dream of life, striving to do what is honourable and right.
Obwaajgan binoojiinh ge-ni-bwaadang bmaadziwin, kina gegoo wii-gwyako-doodang.

NARRATOR / GAA-NIIGAANAAN'GIDOOD

August 5, 1952, Francis Pegahmagabow is laid to rest.
Mnoomini-Giizis naano-gon'gizi, gii-n'go'gaaza Bnaaswi Pegahmagabow.

Here is a story that does not end, but continues today in those who believe in a country where justice will prevail, as new generations rise up to fill the footsteps of warriors who have fallen long ago, whose sacrifices and legacies we continue to remember and honour each November across our vast home and Native land.
Gaawiin shkaasesinoon maanda dbaajmowin, geyaabi go nongwa eyaamgak maa giw edebwewendangig maampii Kiing wii-dbaaknigaadeg, ge-zhi-bzig-wiiwag giw Shki-nishnaabeg wii-noopnanaawaan niw mnisnoon mewnzha gaa-bngishinijin, wii-mkwendming kina gegoo gaa-miigwewaad miinwaa gaa-zhichgewaad gye dash wii-mnaajtooying endso-Gashkadno-Giisoong kina ngoji Gdakiimnaang.

FRANCIS / BNAAWSI

(Francis reaches out slowly to touch the Deer Spirit.)
(Negaaj ezhi-nkenitwaad Waawaashkesh-Mnidoon.)

In my dream I see a beautiful deer, head raised, nose up, ears twitching.
Nbwaanaa waawaashkesh gwenaajwid, shpikweni, shpijaaneni, jjiibtawgeni.

I approach from downwind, but it turns to me, and I realize this is meant to be.
Ninaaskawaa maa niisaanmak, bi-gwekgaabwi ji-waabmid, mii dash iw gii-kendmaan waa-zhiwebak.

133

It is a spirit, a Manido in the body of a deer.
Mnidoowi, aw Mnidoo ezhnaagzid waawaashkeshing.

(Addressing the deer.)
(genoonaad waawaashkeshan.)

I know who you are.
Gkenimin.

The End
Mii sa iw

First performance of Sounding Thunder *at the Festival of the Sound in Parry Sound, Ontario. From left to right: Brian McInnes, Mark Fewer, James Campbell, Waawaate Fobister, James McKay, Larry Beckwith, Jodi Baker Contin, Beverley Johnston, Jennifer Kreisberg, Guy Few, Rachel Thomas and Joel Quarrington. Photo courtesy of Tim Corlis.*

The history of war
is the history of mankind.

– Conrad Aiken, *The Soldier: A Poem,* 1944

AFTERWORD / SHKWAACH KIDWINAN

In 2016, I met the Canadian conductor and musician Larry Beckwith in a café in Toronto to discuss a project that the Festival of the Sound in Parry Sound, Ontario, under the artistic directorship of James Campbell, wanted to produce to mark the festival's thirty-fifth anniversary. Their idea was to showcase a musical based on the life of the highly decorated Ojibwe-Anishnaabe WWI snipper Francis Pegahmagabow, who had lived nearby on Wasauksing, Parry Island. Tim Corlis, the composer, was already engaged for the project, and now they were looking for someone who could write the libretto. Somehow my name had come up through a recommendation. Although I had written in other dramatic and poetic forms, I had never written a libretto, and frankly all I knew about Francis Pegahmagabow was that his achievements in WWI were legendary, and that he had been respected by the military and the general Canadian public alike. What the producers had in mind was to create a production with the same kind of instrumentation as Stravinsky's *The Soldier's Tale*, which they intended to produce at the same venue. As it turned out, the overwhelming reception to *Sounding Thunder: The Song of Francis Pegahmagabow* made their plan for a combined production untenable. It would go on to fly on its own.

I have to say that I was initially hesitant because neither Tim Corlis, the composer, nor the producers are Indigenous. However, as Larry Beckwith explained, Truth and Reconciliation was central to the project, and in that light having a non-Indigenous classical composer and an Indigenous poet-storyteller made sense. Furthermore, I learned that the Festival of the Sound was in contact with the Pegahmagabow family, and they welcomed the project. Adhering to protocol, doing it the right way, made the project all the more inviting to me, and I signed on. Numerous telephone calls between Tim Corlis and me followed, in which we embraced the spirit of collaboration. We were both eager to bring on board more Indigenous artists to tell Francis's story, and we were soon on our way to Wasauksing First Nation on Parry Island, Francis's home community, to meet with the Pegahmagabow family. Members of the family soon became involved – Brian McInnes, Francis's great-great-grandson, became indispensable to the project, and Laura Pegahmagabow become our resident Elder. We had our first production on the reserve in 2018 to a standing ovation. From there *Sounding Thunder* went on to do a limited tour before closing down due of COVID-19. It has since been revived.

What I have done then is present a version of the production written for the page with additional material – a hybrid of sources and forms – to create a dialectic with the original libretto. In this way *The Dialogues* consist of a conversation with the poetic-narrative *Sounding Thunder: The Song of Francis Pegahmagabow* and by implication the reader. One might say the additional material serves to fill in the spaces between the words of the libretto, originally filled by the music in the production, and moves the text in all kinds of novel directions. Surprising even to me. In saying this I have tried to keep the poetry of the libretto in its original form as much as possible with some necessary restructuring for translation. To express the intention of this book, in the spirit of Truth and Reconciliation, I have woven Indigenous and Western perspectives throughout the left- and right-hand sides of the page. It is my hope that both sides support and build on each other to create something new and meaningful. I have therefore also included an Anishnaabemowin-Ojibwe translation of the original *Sounding Thunder: The Song of Francis Pegahmagabow* text from the stage production, pushing my intervention as much as I can. As an aside, it is interesting to note that up until the nineteenth century, a time when Indigenous peoples were swamped by an influx of new immigrants and pushed out of the way and onto reserves and into the backcountry, settlers (and certainly Indigenous peoples) speaking an Indigenous language were not out of the ordinary. As it stands today Indigenous languages in Canada are desperately in need of support if they are to survive. It is my sincere hope that language learners will benefit from this book.

A note on orthography and terminology: Readers will notice different orthographies for the Ojibwe language; this distinct feature reflects regional dialects. Readers will also see that I have used the word "Indian" throughout the text. Indigenous peoples have a complicated relationship with English and with this word in particular. There are individuals and communities that still use it, just as there are individuals and communities who find it pejorative. I have used it here in textual context and it is a word that Francis Pegahmagabow himself used when speaking English as indicated in his letters.

Lastly, a note on the excerpts within the book: In some instances I have not used quotation marks, indicated idiosyncratic spellings or omissions of text within an excerpt due to the demands of poetry. If using this text for academic purposes, I suggest checking excerpts against original sources.

Miigwech,

Armand Garnet Ruffo
Kingston, ON, 2024

ACKNOWLEDGEMENTS / MIIGWECHWI'INDWAA

The spirit and legacy of Francis Pegahmagabow and the Indigenous veterans of WWI.

Tim Corlis, composer and collaborator, who became a friend during the process. *Sounding Thunder* could not have happened without him. His sense of humour, goodwill and determination kept the project going. His observations on the first performance were borrowed and combined with my thoughts. I am further grateful to him for letting me include material related to the performance music.

Brian D. McInnes, Ojibwe scholar and brother-in-arms, who contributed his deep knowledge of Ojibwe culture, language and history to the production of *Sounding Thunder*. My deep gratitude to him for his remarkable Anishnaabemowin-Ojibwe translation (any faults are my own) and for letting me contact him at all hours with questions about the Ojibwe language. His own scholarly text *Sounding Thunder: The Stories of Francis Pegahmagabow* was an invaluable resource, which I highly recommend. A further miigwech to the Wasauksing M'tigo Min Trust for their language support.

James Campbell, artistic director of the Festival of the Sound, who recruited me for the project and initially put it all together. Chi-Miigwech for his commitment to *Sounding Thunder*.

Laura Pegahmagabow for her wisdom and humour, and the Pegahmagabow family in general for their generous welcome and support.

Larry Beckwith who met with me in Toronto when *Sounding Thunder* was still an idea and spoke enthusiastically about the project and convinced me to sign on. I am grateful that he did.

The amazing group of musicians, actors and technicians/artists, who contributed to the project at various stages and in various ways to bring *Sounding Thunder* to life.

Adrian Hayes for his necessary book, *Pegahmagabow: Life-Long Warrior*, and to the many other historians and journalists who have written about Francis Pegahmagabow, whose work I drew on.

Writer and researcher Kristen den Hartog who shared her findings about my great-uncles John and Joe E/Spaniel with me, and poet Marilyn Dumont for her positive feedback on an early draft.

To all those who came out to see *Sounding Thunder* and gave it such thunderous support and to those who bring truth to Indigenous peoples' struggles.

My sincere appreciation to Peter Midgley, who took on the job of editing the book at exactly the right time and brought his sensitivity and editorial insight to it. He pushed me to make it a better book. Likewise, my thanks to Managing Editor Ashley Hisson at Wolsak & Wynn for her sharp eye and detailed comments.

Finally, my heartfelt miigwech to Noelle Allen and everyone at Wolsak & Wynn for their continued support and generosity. Publishing a book with a good chunk of it translated into Anishnaabemowin-Ojibwe takes courage.

Versions of "For the Last 340 (or so) Colossal North Atlantic Right Whales" and "Resting II" appeared in *ARC* 100 (Spring 2023). The Ontario Arts Council and the Canada Council for the Arts provided support.

TRANSLATOR'S NOTE / GAA-AAN'KINOOTMAAGED ZHIBII'GEWIN

Nishnaabemwin, the language of the Ojibwe, Odawa and Potawatomi peoples of Georgian Bay (Mnidoo-gamii – The Lake of the Spirit), was the first language of Francis Pegahmagabow. Spoken by the Nishnaabeg ("the good beings") throughout the Great Lakes region and beyond in both Canada and the United States, the Nishnaabeg recognize their language as a sacred gift from the Spirit, which embodies their original values, worldview and unique ways of thought.

Presenting this work in Francis's first language was an honour and also an act of linguistic justice. Hundreds of years of active colonial presence have decimated the vibrancy of spoken Nishnaabemwin in its homeland. This Nishnaabemwin translation is therefore meant to support the dynamic language revitalization movement of the present. It is the language that the land, water and spirit of this place best understands.

The specialized English language terminology of Armand's poetic-prose narrative presented several unique challenges for translation. This is far from everyday Ojibwe. However, Nishnaabemwin is a highly adaptive language that matches the resilience and adaptive capacity of Indigenous nations. The productive capacity of it provided a way for me to give expression to even the most nuanced English writing. While this is not a classic translation initiative, and by no means perfect, it represents a bold new foray into expressive language use and representation.

A few unique pronunciation features of the double-vowel system are highlighted below.

VOWELS
Nishnaabemwin is written with seven vowels, three short vowels and four long vowels. The following chart lists some English language words that have similar sounds.

Short vowels		Long vowels	
a	"but"	aa	"saw"
i	"pit"	ii	"key" or "see"
o	"okay"	oo	"coat"
		e	"leg" or "flag"

GLOTTAL STOP

A glottal stop is caused by a momentary pause or stoppage of breath. This is written in Nishnaabemwin with an apostrophe as in de' ("heart") or wen'enh ("namesake"). This is a similar sound as found in the English expression "uh-oh."

Armand Garnet Ruffo is an Anishnaabe writer from northern Ontario and a member of the Chapleau (Fox Lake) Cree First Nation. A recipient of an Honorary Life Membership Award from the League of Canadian Poets and the Latner Griffin Writers' Trust Poetry Prize, he is recognized as a major contributor to both Indigenous literature and Indigenous literary scholarship in Canada. His publications *Norval Morrisseau: Man Changing into Thunderbird* (2014) and *Treaty #* (2019) were finalists for Governor General's Literary Awards. He teaches at Queen's University in Kingston, Ontario.

Brian D. McInnes is the great-grandson of Francis Pegahmagabow and a member of the Wasauksing First Nation. He is an author and professor of Ojibwe language and culture in the American Indian Studies program at the University of Wisconsin–Madison. His extensive knowledge about the life of his great-grandfather and his Ojibwe culture and language informed the production of *Sounding Thunder: The Song of Francis Pegahmagabow.*